Cake Decorating

An A–Z of hints and tips

Pat Lock

MEREHURST

**To John, for his continual help
over the years**

Published 1990 by Merehurst Limited,
Ferry House, 51–57 Lacy Road, Putney,
London SW15 1PR

Copyright © Merehurst Limited 1990

ISBN 1 85391 171 2

Edited by Bridget Jones
Designed by Jo Tapper
Cover artwork by Jill Newton
Illustrations by Joyce Tuhill
Typeset by Medcalf Type Ltd, Bicester, Oxon

Printed in Great Britain by
Mackays of Chatham plc, Chatham, Kent

The author and publishers would like to thank Squires Kitchen
School of Cake Decorating, The Potteries, Pottery Lane,
Wrecclesham, Farnham, Surrey GU10 4QJ for the loan of
equipment.

Note: A standard spoon measurement is used throughout.
1 teaspoon = one 5ml spoon.
All spoon measures are level.
Ovens should be preheated to specified temperature.
Eggs are standard (size 3) unless otherwise stated.
Follow either metric, Imperial or cup measures (where given)
as quantities are not interchangeable.

FOREWORD

During many years of teaching cake decorating, I have come across all sorts of difficulties that students encounter, from the problem of achieving a perfectly smooth coat of royal icing on a Christmas cake late on Christmas eve to learning how to make a piping bag which doesn't fall apart. The popular craft of modelling flowers also brings its own share of problems.

So often beginners are afraid to attempt creative skills because they feel that they are not artistic. All cake decorators have had to start at the beginning, learning by trial and error. It helps if you have an artistic flair but with practice, patience and perseverance you can achieve success with cake decorating skills. At the same time you will gain a great deal of pleasure, as well as discovering a pride in your work. A decorated cake always gives enormous happiness to the recipient, whether it is a novelty cake for a child, a chocolate gâteau for a favourite relative or the ultimate wedding cake.

I would like to think you will dip into this book not only when confronted with a problem but also when you are looking out for new ideas. Hopefully the hints and tips that I have included will avoid time-consuming mistakes and make cake decorating as enjoyable as possible.

Have fun!

Pat Lock

ACETATE
See papers, coverings and wrappings*.

AIRBRUSH

A precision artist's instrument, which consists of a brush attached to a compressor by a hose. A small cup above the brush is used to hold food colour. A finger trigger regulates the flow of air from the compressor through the hose, cup of colour and a tiny nozzle in the brush to give a fine, even spray. Thin lines are made by holding the nozzle close to the surface and applying gentle pressure on the trigger. By holding the nozzle further away and using more pressure an area of overall colour is achieved. The colour is sprayed on a dry iced surface. Designs or pictures may be created on a cake. Sugar flowers made in white icing may be sprayed with various colours.

The technique is a quick one; however the equipment is expensive and most people require a lot of practice to achieve a reasonable standard, particularly for spraying artistic scenes on cakes. For artists or artistic cake decorators, it is an alternative method for creating elaborate cake designs.

Remember . . .
Check that the canister of compressed air is full enough to complete the decoration. It's a good idea to keep a spare canister.

ALBUMEN POWDER

Dried pasteurised egg white in the form of a powder. When dissolved in water it reconstitutes to egg whites and can be used to make royal icing* or meringues.

There are two types: the more readily available, and less

expensive, fortified albumen (with added starch and other ingredients) is pale cream in colour and it dissolves easily. Pure hen albumen is a slightly deeper colour cream and it requires more care when mixed with water to ensure it dissolves completely. Both are suitable for use in royal icing. However, the pure hen albumen gives greater bulk to the icing and it is stronger, therefore more suitable for run outs*. The advantages of using albumen powder is that there are no leftover yolks or risk of infection from salmonella bacteria which may be present in raw eggs.
Quantities: 22 g (¾ oz/11 teaspoons) albumen powder to 155 ml (5 fl oz/⅔ cup) water. For a smaller amount use 1 teaspoon albumen powder to 1 tablespoon water.

Use

Place the required amount of lukewarm water in a grease-free bowl (glass, china or metal). Using a fine nylon sieve, sift the albumen into the bowl, whisking well all the time. Whisk until the whites are frothy. Use a clean wooden spoon to gradually beat in sifted icing (confectioner's) sugar.

> **Secrets of Success**
> *If the albumen powder does not dissolve immediately, leave it to stand for a few hours, then whisk it again.*

AMERICAN FROSTING

Frosting is quick to make and easily applied to the cake. The frosting sets quickly with a crisp crust and it has a smooth texture, produced by boiling the syrup to the correct temperature. Frosting is made by whisking sugar syrup into egg whites. Care must be taken when boiling sugar. Use a small heavy saucepan to make the syrup and melt the sugar over a low heat until it has dissolved completely. Raise the heat and boil the syrup to 116°c (240°F). *Do not stir the syrup while it boils* otherwise it will form white crystals. As soon as the syrup is at the right temperature whisk it into the egg whites. See crème au beurre* for temperature test.

Use

Swirl frosting on plain cakes and Victoria sandwich cakes. Have the cake ready as the frosting sets quickly once made.

Colour and flavour

Frosting is usually left plain white but it can be flavoured by adding coffee essence or cocoa powder dissolved to a smooth thin paste in hot water. Add the flavouring while whisking in the sugar syrup.

> **Secrets of Success**
> *If the syrup splashes up the sides of the pan as it boils, sugar crystals will form on the hot pan and drop back into the syrup. These may cause the rest of the syrup to crystallize in which case it will become useless. Keep a cup of water and a pastry brush at hand, then brush the inside of the pan with a very little water to prevent any syrup from forming crystals. When whisking the syrup into the egg whites, use dry, warmed blades in the food mixer. Pour the syrup into the bowl avoiding the blades otherwise it can turn into a sticky mess.*

ANGELICA

The crystallized stalk from the plant of that name. Angelica grows well in this country and the stalks may be crystallized (or candied) at home but it is a long process, taking about fourteen days.

Commercial angelica is sold in strips and it is often coated in excess sugar. Food colour is also added to most types.

Use

As a decoration on informal cakes, usually with American frosting*, buttercream* and chocolate*. Cut diagonally, angelica is used to resemble leaves.

> **Quick Tip**
> *Soak angelica very briefly in hot water to make it pliable and to remove surplus sugar. Dry well before use.*

ANGLES

If you are confused by the various angles referred to in cake decorating instructions, buy a small plastic protractor and draw the angles on paper. Use the drawing as a visual guide. As a rough guide, a perfectly 'square' corner, or upright, has an angle of 90°. An icing ruler held at 45° would come halfway between the flat surface and the upright of a square corner.

APRICOT GLAZE

Apricot glaze is made by boiling apricot jam, then sieving it to remove pieces of fruit. The glaze should be used while it is warm. Bring the jam to the boil in a small saucepan over low heat, then sieve it into a bowl. Apricot jam is used for its delicate flavour which complements marzipan*. Strongly flavoured fruit jams would give the finished cake a distinct taste. Red jam shows up when the cake is cut. Sieved jelly marmalade may be used instead.

Use
The glaze is brushed over cakes before applying marzipan. The jam sets and keeps the marzipan firmly in place. It is also used as a coating for fresh or canned fruit, for example when decorating gâteaux*.

Keeping Qualities
Make apricot glaze in small quantities as you need it. Any leftovers may be stored in a covered container in the refrigerator and used up quickly. Do not return the glaze to the jam pot – it is likely to have small crumbs in it and it is no longer sterile so it will not keep as well as jam.

Quick Tip
Cheaper jams contain less fruit and are more suitable for making a glaze. Some jams which contain very few pieces of fruit may be boiled and used without sieving. The jam must be boiled and perfectly clean utensils should be used to prevent any risk of a mould forming between the marzipan and cake.

BAKING TINS

Heavy-duty, well-made tins will last for years and they will promote even cooking. Heat penetration through thin, inferior tins can result in cakes with overcooked sides. Strong tins have even bases which will not warp. Cake decorating shops often hire out good-quality tins, including those of unusual and novelty shapes. Adjustable tins are also available.

Preparing Tins
• For rich fruit cake*, line the tin with one or two thicknesses of greaseproof paper. Tie a piece of brown paper or corrugated paper around the outside of the tin.
• For Victoria sandwich cake*, base-line the tins.
• For Madeira cake* (pound cake), line the tin with one thickness of greaseproof paper.
• For fatless sponge*, ensure the tin is evenly greased and given a dusting of flour. Do not mark the interior of the prepared tin with your fingers – one small uncoated area will make the sponge stick.
• For small cakes, place double-thick paper cake cases in patty tins. This will keep the cakes in shape as they cook.

Lining Tins
Grease the tin before lining with paper. When lining with two layers of paper, grease the first layer to keep the second layer in place. The paper should stand about 3 cm (1½ in) above the top of the tin.

Measuring the Volume of Tins
Measure the volume of a tin to decide on the quantity of mixture required. Take a tin for which the quantity is known and fill it with water. Pour the water into the tin you wish to use, then measure the volume of water. If the second tin holds less water, reduce the quantities of cake mixture proportionally; increase the quantities if the tin holds more water.

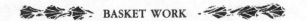

Baking Frames

These are tins without a base, which makes it difficult to judge the quantity of mixture required. A foolproof method is to stand the tin on a level work surface and line it with a large waterproof plastic bag. Pour the water into the lined frame, then compare the volume with that held in a standard tin and note if more, or less, mixture is necessary.

BASKET WORK

Can be piped in royal icing* over marzipan* on a rich fruit cake*, or in stiff buttercream* on a Victoria sandwich or Madeira cake* (pound cake). Royal icing needs to be well beaten to achieve sufficient bulk to hold its shape and it should be put in a medium piping bag.

Use stiff buttercream (*not* made with soft margarine) to ensure that the pattern shows in the cream. To pipe buttercream, use a bag made with two layers of paper, or you may find it easier to use several small bags, discarding them when they need refilling.

Icing Tube (Tip)

Use an icing tube (tip) specially designed for this work. The basket work tube (tip) has a flat piping end with both, or sometimes only one, edge finely serrated. A star tube (tip) may be used but it does not give such a realistic effect.

Piping Technique

The most commonly used method is to pipe both the horizontal and vertical strokes with the basket work tube (tip). This way, a large area can be covered with each line and with some practice you will soon become accomplished.

Alternatively, the vertical lines may be piped with a writing tube (tip) and the horizontal lines piped with the basket tube (tip). This method takes longer and care is needed to keep the piping neat but it results in a very realistic appearance.

Basket Work Designs

The technique is normally used to create a basket of flowers, with moulded flowers* on top and a tilted lid. Depending on the number of flowers available, the lid can be raised on both sides with flowers underneath or tilted to one side to show fewer

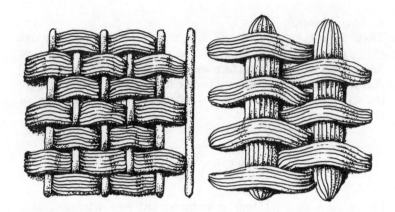

Left: basket work piped using a basket work tube (tip) and a writing tube (tip).
Right: using only the basket work tube (tip).

flowers. Basket work may also be used for a hat design, with a cluster of flowers at the front of the brim and flowing sugarpaste or ribbon streamers at the back.

> **Quick Tip**
> *On a basket of flowers, glue a piece of smooth foil to one side of a cardboard lid and pipe the basket work decoration on the other side. Leave the icing to dry and place the lid in position over the flowers with the foil down. The reflection of the flowers on the foil will add to the beauty and colour of the design.*

BAS RELIEF

A form of three-dimensional sugarcraft sculpture, with the design standing proud of the background. Bas relief can be modelled directly on the cake surface or made on a plaque. The outline is traced directly on the firm, dry iced surface. Layers of sugarpaste* are moulded within the outline to build up the three-dimensional shape.

If a figure is modelled, make any covering of clothes from pastillage* as this may be rolled out thinly and draped into material-like folds, pleats or flounces.

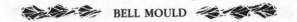

BELL MOULD

An extremely useful mould, available in metal or plastic and in a variety of sizes.

Use
To make bells as decoration for a wedding or celebration cake, with sugar or silk flowers spilling out. Also used to make decorations for Christmas cakes. Cut in half, the bells can be applied flat against the sides of cakes.

A bell mould may also be used to shape novelty figures. Long gowns are the perfect covering for the shape, such as on a choir boy, angel or Father Christmas.

Sugar Bells
Made in the same way as sand pies! Slightly dampen caster sugar with water. To test for the correct consistency, squeeze some dampened sugar in a tightly closed fist and it should show finger impressions. Pack the mould, level off the top and immediately turn out the sugar on to a level surface. Once the outside of the sugar shape is dry enough to be picked up, the middle can be scooped out using the handle of a small spoon. Leave the bells to dry in the sun or in a warm room.

Secrets of Success
Granulated sugar may be used – the bell will not have such a smooth surface as those made with caster sugar but the larger sugar crystals add a sparkle. Wipe out the mould with absorbent kitchen paper after moulding each bell, to remove any damp sugar that is clinging to it.

Coloured Bells
Colour can be worked into the sugar using the fingertips or the water may be coloured. Remember that the sugar will reduce the strength of the colour.

Lace Bells
Grease the outside of a bell mould with white vegetable fat. Using royal icing* and a no. 0 or 1 writing tube (tip), pipe a design of trellis* or cornelli* work over the mould. When dry place near a source of heat to melt the grease, then carefully slip the bell off the mould.

11

Piped Bells

Use a writing tube (tip) and royal icing. Pipe large dots on waxed* or non-stick paper*. While the icing is still wet, pipe smaller dots on top. When the outsides of the bells are firm enough to handle, the centre can be scooped out with a thin, sharp implement.

> **Secrets of Success**
> *To pipe bells with a perfect circular base, keep the point of the tube (tip) down inside the blob of icing. The blob of icing will then grow in size from the middle, keeping the edges neat.*

Moulded Bells

Use pastillage* and work a small piece until smooth and free of cracks. Form the pastillage into a rounded, bell-like shape, about half the size of the bell mould. Dust the surface of the paste and the inside of the mould with cornflour (corn starch). Place the rounded end of the paste into the mould and keep smoothing it gently with your fingers and thumb into the centre of the mould until the paste completely covers the inside of the mould. The paste should be thinner towards the edge. Take the bell out of the mould occasionally to ensure the paste is not sticking. Remove any excess paste around the edge by pressing firmly against the rim of the mould.

BLOSSOM CUTTER

Used to make small flowers which are useful as an individual decoration as well as for combining with larger blossoms. Cutters may be made of metal or plastic and they are used to stamp out flowers in one piece. Some cutters are of the plunger type, incorporating a spring-loaded plunger to curve the flower once it is stamped out.

Stamping Out Flowers

Roll out either sugarpaste* or pastillage*. The latter may be rolled thinly to make finer flowers. Use the chosen blossom cutter to stamp out the shapes and immediately place them on a piece of foam. Use a modelling tool* with a rounded end to depress the centre of the flower – this makes the petals curve upwards slightly and look natural.

Varying textures of foam will give a different curve to the

flowers depending on how easily it compresses when pressed. Lightly dust the surface of the foam with cornflour (corn starch) to prevent the blossoms from sticking.

Plunger Flowers
The plunger cutter with a spring mechanism is quicker to use. Stamp out the flower from the rolled-out paste, then hold the cutter over the foam and depress the spring plunger. The flower will be pushed out of the cutter and the plunger curves the petals at the same time.

BLOSSOM TINTS

Also known as petal dust and dusting powder. Fine powders in pale and deep colours. Used for dusting on flowers or a dry iced surface to give a background tint or variation in shades of colour. They are also useful for dusting the edge of frills. Different powders may be mixed to create a wide variety of colours. Silver and gold lustre add a glamorous sparkle to celebration cakes.

Using Blossom Tints
They may be used to colour royal icing* but this is an expensive method best reserved for matching the icing to a dusted decoration.

When piping coloured lace work*, it is better to add powder to royal icing instead of paste colours which generally contain glycerine. They attract moisture from the atmosphere and, in turn, this could soften the lace slightly on standing.

Blossom tints are useful for colouring white chocolate, for example to make moulded roses. Liquid colour is not suitable as it reacts with the chocolate to spoil the texture, causing it to stiffen.

Applying Blossom Tints
A common complaint is that the powder will not stick to the dry icing. This can be due to the fact that there is insufficient powder on the brush. Use a good-quality brush with a rounded end; cheap brushes do not pick up enough powder. Place some blossom tint on a flat surface and load the brush by bouncing it on its side in the powder. When the brush is well loaded apply the powder to the area to be coloured.

> **Secrets of Success**
> *To soften the colour of a dark blossom tint, mix in a little white blossom tint. If cornflour (corn starch) or icing (confectioner's) sugar are used the tint does not adhere as thoroughly to the surface of the icing.*

BOARDS

The important point to remember when buying boards is to have the right size and thickness for the cake. If possible try to reflect the shape of the cake by using the same shape of board.

Weight
A light cake can be placed on a thin gâteau board or cake card. Heavy fruit cakes need a cake drum, either 1 cm (½ in) or 1.4 cm (⅝ in) thick. Extra large, heavy cakes are best put on two boards of the same size which are stuck together with icing. Attach board edging to cover the seam.

Size
Buy boards at least 5–7.5 cm (2–3 in) bigger than the cakes. This will keep your hands away from the sides of the cakes, avoiding damaging the icing and decoration as you lift the cakes. Boards used for wedding cakes* must balance with the depth as well as the width of the cakes. Very deep cakes require boards about 13 cm (5 in) larger than their size.

A cake decorated with collars* will require a cake board at least 10 cm (4 in) larger than its size. This will enable the cake to be

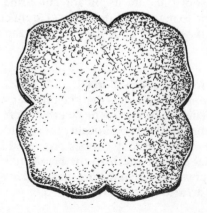

A useful shape of board for either square or round cakes.

lifted up without damaging the collar, also the wider board will balance the width of the collar.

Shapes
Gone are the days when boards were either round or square; now they are available in many different shapes. They match the shapes of baking tins, for example petal shaped, heart shaped, hexagonal, oval and others.

Covering Boards
Shapes can be cut out of chipboard and covered in embossed silver or gold paper (available from cake decorating suppliers). The easiest way to cover a board is to lay the paper upside down on a clean firm surface. Place the board on top and draw around it. Allow extra paper outside the shape for the depth of the board plus 1 cm (½ in) to turn under.

Paste the paper, leaving the edge unpasted, and place the board on the centre of it. Carefully slide the board to the edge of the table and use the palm of your hand to press the paper against the sides of the board. Turn the excess paper neatly over the board edges.

On a round board, make cuts in the paper at 5 cm (2 in) intervals so that it sticks flat on the base.

For squared boards, or other shapes with corners, make slits into the corners of the paper. Paste and press down the overlapping sections neatly.

Cut out a piece of white paper slightly smaller than the board and paste it on the base to cover the edges of embossed paper. Allow the board to dry before use.

Quick Tip
Do not use cooking foil to cover boards – it tears very easily.

BOUGHT DECORATIONS

Most cake decorating suppliers offer a wide variety of high-quality, ready-made decorations. Use them creatively to enhance simple cakes, avoiding having to practise techniques which are unfamiliar, or simply to save time. Here are just a few examples.

Bride and Groom Top Decoration: Not considered fashionable by many brides; however, some are very pretty.

Crystallized Flowers: Many varieties are available and they are usually sold by weight.

Crystallized or Candied Orange or Lemon Slices: Useful as a decoration on buttercream*. These vary from 'jellied' sugar-coated orange and lemon decorations to slices of fruit that have been candied (recognize these by their size) and may be cut up.

Dragee: A small, hard sugar ball available in colours but usually silver. The surface of dragees can melt if placed on moist icing.

Heather Sprays: Attractive for decorating a man's cake as they are not too feminine.

Pastillage Flowers: Expensive due to the time involved in making them. Usually sold in a spray, they add a professional touch to a cake covered with sugarpaste* or royal icing*.

Piped Flowers: Royal icing flowers are available in many varieties and colours. Useful when time is short or if you are not skilled at piping flowers. May be used on formal cakes.

Silk Flowers: A quick, attractive form of decoration. Place different shapes together to create interesting sprays and add some small flowers. As well as those on sale in cake decorating shops, look out for flower sprays in gift shops and garden centres. Large sprays may be split to give lots of tiny flower heads.

Silver Horseshoes: Not particularly fashionable; however, they are used on simple cakes. Made in different sizes, the smaller ones may be added discreetly as part of piped decorations.

BRIAR ROSES

These flowers are easy to make. Use a briar rose cutter to cut the petals to make briar roses. Available in different sizes, a cutter will always give a better result than a template because of the sharp cutting edge.

Do not cut too many petals out at once or they will dry out. Soften the edges of the petals with a modelling tool* to thin and gently flute them. Place in a mould to dry. Lift some of the petals in the mould and place tiny balls of plastic wrap between the petals. This will make the flowers look more lifelike. When dry, use tweezers to remove the balls of plastic wrap.

Making a Mould
Cut out a 7.5 cm (3 in) circle of greaseproof* or non-stick* paper. Fold the paper into four and crease the folds. Open out and cut

along one of the creases to the centre of the paper. Overlap the two cut edges and stick down. The mould can be adjusted to make it smaller or larger by reducing or increasing the overlap.

Stamens

The stamens need to be added with care. The quickest way to make a flower centre is to press a small ball of paste on a piece of tulle, or on a nylon sieve, to make an impression of the pattern. Place this paste in the centre of the rose.

Commercial stamens need to be curved to follow the movement of the petals. Take a few stamens, fold them in two and bend their stalks over your forefinger before cutting off the excess stem.

Quick Tip

Yellow cotton makes very realistic stamens. Wind the cotton about sixty times around the end of a pencil. Slide the cotton off and slip a piece of thin wire through the centre hole, then twist it together securely. Tie a double thickness of cotton around the base of the shank of cotton, as near to the wire as possible. This will keep the threads together. Cut the opposite end of the loop of threads, curving the cut down slightly at either side. Moisten the tip of the threads and dip them carefully into brown food colouring or cocoa powder.

BRIDGE WORK

The basis for extension work*, bridge work supports the lines of icing (curtain work*) keeping them away from the cake.

Bridge work is a technique for the more experienced decorator. It takes time, patience, good eyesight and a steady hand. It is the name given to the overpiped scalloping that lies under the vertically piped curtain work which makes up the completed edging known as extension work.

Marking the Scallops

Cut a template to the exact size and shape of the scallops to fit the cake. The marked line for the scallops should leave sufficient space for a row of small shells to be piped around the base of the cake.

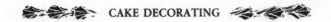

Piping Bridge Work

Pipe a row of shells around the base of the cake and leave to dry. Pipe the first line of icing on the scallops and leave to dry before attempting to pipe another row on top. Leave each row to dry otherwise the built-up scallop could collapse.

The choice of writing tube (tip) to pipe the lines depends on your skill, the time available and patience.

Secrets of Success
Once the bridge work is dry, carefully brush thinned-down royal icing over it to strengthen any weak areas.

BRODERIE ANGLAISE

An embroidery technique which forms a successful basis for a cake decorating design. Small holes of different shapes are cut into soft paste and later royal icing* is piped around them. The designs are marked and cut in thinly rolled sugarpaste*. The paste is then applied to the surface of an iced cake. Broderie anglaise work and the ribbon insertion* technique go together well.

Equipment

Sets of cutters may be bought to stamp out designs, giving a sharp, exact cut out. Alternatively, holes can be made with a knitting needle, the end of a writing tube (tip), aspic cutters, a tiny blossom cutter or a metal skewer.

Uses
• On a frill around a cake.
• As bands of embroidery on the top or around the side of a cake.
• To decorate a bib for a christening cake.
• To surround a plaque*.

Applying Broderie Anglaise to a Cake
Be careful not to stretch the paste when picking it up. It is a good idea to roll out the paste on a thin piece of card and use this to assist in lifting the paste.

Piping

When the paste is dry, use a fine writing tube (tip) to pipe fine lines close to the edge of each cut out shape. Use the same tube (tip) to pipe a linking pattern of embroidery work directly on the surface of the paste. Use a fine, damp paint brush to take away any surplus ends of icing.

> **Design Idea**
> *Stamp out broderie anglaise shapes on a piece of white sugarpaste, trimmed to loosely overhang the cake like a tablecloth. Arrange this as an overlay on a base covering of coloured sugarpaste.*

BRUSH EMBROIDERY

A technique used mainly to create floral designs. A piped royal icing* outline is brushed inwards while still soft, to resemble petals and leaves.

Marking the Design

Trace the design on greaseproof paper* or non-stick paper*. Hold the paper firmly on top of the iced cake or plaque* and scribe the design through the paper.

> **Quick Tip**
> *Use a lipstick pencil to trace over the outline showing through on the back of the paper. Place on cake with the lipstick lines underneath and draw the outline on top using a HB pencil.*

Semi-Permanent Transfer

Use for embossing designs on a soft sugarpaste* or pastillage* surface. Trace the reverse image of the design on firm card. Use a no. 1 icing tube (tip) and royal icing to outline the pattern, erasing any ends of icing with a fine, damp paint brush. Leave to dry. Press into the surface of soft sugarpaste or pastillage to make an impression of the piped design.

Instead of piping on card, place the drawn design under a piece of glass or perspex and pipe the outline to use as above.

Piping and Brushing

When piping on the cake, add a small amount of piping gel* to the royal icing to give a smooth texture and to stop it from drying out too quickly.

Always start on the outside edge of the design and work on one section at a time. Pipe the outline and brush it immediately with a dampened brush. The brush must be good quality and have a rounded edge. A brush with a pointed tip will make sharp lines in the icing. Brush the icing down the whole of the petal to cover it completely with a thin film. Pipe areas of the flower or design that are meant to be further away thinly, and the foreground area slightly thicker. This gives a three-dimensional effect.

Colour

Pipe using white icing. Moisten the brush with coloured water to achieve a variegated effect. Alternatively, once dry the brush embroidery can be dusted with blossom tint*. Brush embroidery designs show up well by piping white on a coloured base.

> **Quick Tip**
> *When practising this technique, pipe in icing coloured differently from the base. This way you will be able to see if you are brushing the icing correctly.*

BUTTERCREAM

Also known as butter icing. Buttercream is made by creaming sifted icing sugar with either unsalted butter or soft margarine. This may be done by hand or by using a food mixer. The longer the buttercream is beaten the lighter it will become, both in colour and texture, as more air is incorporated.

Equal quantities of fat and sugar will give a buttercream which is easy to use both as a coating and for piping.

Uses

Buttercream can be used to fill cakes and to coat the top and sides of gâteaux*. It can also be used to cover and decorate small fancies. A smooth, thin undercoat of buttercream may be spread on cakes before they are covered with sugarpaste*. As a general rule, depending on the depth of the cake, 250 g (8 oz) fat and 250 g (8 oz) icing sugar will make sufficient buttercream to fill and coat the top and sides of a 20 cm (8 in) round cake, leaving enough for piping a simple border.

Colour and Flavour

When colouring buttercream, you may like to complement the flavour with a matching shade. For example, pale green with peppermint, yellow with lemon juice and finely grated peel. Alternatively, vanilla essence gives a good flavour. Lemon curd blends well with buttercream to give a delicate flavour.

Melted chocolate can be added but do make sure the buttercream is at room temperature otherwise the chocolate may set as it is mixed in. If this does happen, gently warm the buttercream over hot water to soften the chocolate, mix well, then leave until it cools to a usable consistency. Coffee, chocolate and cocoa powder impart both colour and flavour.

Secrets of Success
Do not add dry cocoa powder to buttercream. Blend 1–2 tablespoons cocoa powder with a little hot water to make a smooth, creamy paste. When cool, add to the buttercream. This method ensures a superior flavour.

Applying Buttercream to Cakes

The buttercream must be at room temperature. If it is too firm it will pull crumbs away from the cake. Soften the buttercream by beating it over warm water or beat in a very small amount of hot water. The buttercream must be soft enough to spread easily. Use a firm palette knife and first coat the top of the cake with a smooth layer of buttercream, then lift the cake on the palm of your hand and carefully spread buttercream around the side. A second coat may be applied if necessary, in which case chill the first layer of buttercream to firm up first.

Piping with Buttercream

Use an open star tube (tip) and a large piping bag. Buttercream is the easiest medium to use for piping. However, when piping a large area buttercream may begin to melt from the heat of the hands. To combat this use two thicknesses of paper when making the piping bag or use a fabric bag. Keep your hands as cool as possible.

If a paper piping bag softens around the nozzle the edge of the paper can slip between the grooves in the nozzle. This 'smudges' the piping so that the pattern does not show clearly. If the buttercream is too warm the piping will not have a clearly defined pattern.

Decorating Ideas

Apply the design to the top of the cake first. Use a palette knife held with the index finger firmly placed on the blade.

Swirled Effect: Draw the tip of the knife through the buttercream swirling it from side to side.

Snow Scene: Use the back of the knife to pull up the buttercream into peaks.

Ridges: Use the handle of a spoon to make ridges in the buttercream, working in diamond or square patterns.

Serrated Scraper: Use this to make fine, even ridges around the side or over the top of a cake.

Freezing

Freeze for up to 3 months. Take buttercream out of the freezer the day before it is needed and soften once defrosted.

BUTTERCREAM ROSES

Make up a stiff buttercream* using unsalted butter and double the quantity of icing sugar to butter. Follow the instructions for piped flowers*. A pretty effect is obtained by using buttercream in two shades, placed side by side in the piping bag, to make a variegated rose.

Leave the roses to firm up in the refrigerator before placing them carefully on the cake. To use the roses straight away, cut out circles of thin marzipan* and slide these up the cocktail stick to form the base of the rose. Pale green marzipan bases make an attractive addition to the roses.

Freezing

Open freeze the roses on their backing paper, on a baking tray lined with plastic wrap. Store in a rigid container. When required, peel off the backing paper and immediately place the frozen roses on the cake. Allow to defrost slowly. This prevents the roses from being damaged.

CAKES

The basis of good cake decorating is to have a well-made cake of a good shape. Like clothes on a fashion model, icing looks good on a cake that has a good shape. It is disappointing if a high standard of decoration is not matched by eating quality. Here are some suggestions that may help with cake making.

Temperature
Keep all ingredients warm. Although recipes use the phrase 'at room temperature', kitchens vary. Consider the heat in a bakery – one reason why the professional baker achieves good results. Warm the bowl and beater in hot water and dry well. Soften the butter or margarine. Never take eggs, butter or margarine straight out of the refrigerator to use, and warm the sugar in the oven for a few minutes.

> ### Secrets of Success
> *Cold eggs can cause the mixture to curdle. To prevent this happening, place whole eggs in a bowl of hand-hot water for about 5 minutes until they are warmed through.*

Eggs
Use the size stated in the recipe or in the notes at the front of some cookbooks. Using a different size will give either more or less liquid in proportion to the dry ingredients and change the consistency of the batter. If the recipe or book does not state a size, use standard size 3.

Tins
Prepare tins before mixing a cake. This is particularly important when making a whisked sponge as the mixture must go into the oven directly it is ready or it will collapse.

For sponges and Victoria sandwich mixtures, buy tins with straight sides and about 3.5 cm (1½ in) deep. This depth will prevent the heat reaching the surface of the cake and causing it to crust over before it has risen properly.

Use the size of tin stated in the recipe. To ensure equal amounts of mixture are put in two tins, add up the total weight of ingredients, then divide the weight by two. Weigh one empty tin, then add this amount to the half weight of ingredients. Place the tin on the scale and add mixture until the total weight is reached.

Remember . . .
Baking more than one cake in the oven will create additional steam and increase the cooking time slightly.

Flour
Always sift flour. This is not just to remove lumps – most flour is not lumpy – it lightens the flour by incorporating air. For example, try sifting a cup full of flour into a basin, then pour the flour back into the cup and you will find that there is some left over. The volume of flour has increased because of the air incorporated.

Chocolate Cakes
Cocoa powder will give a better flavour if it is blended with boiling water, to make a smooth cream, then cooled before adding to the cake mixture.

Melted chocolate gives a delicious flavour but because of its weight and fat content the resulting cake is usually of the heavier type and not as well risen as those flavoured with cocoa powder.

Keeping Qualities
• One-stage cake or quick-mix cake will keep for about 5 days but it dries out gradually because extra baking powder is used.
• Whisked sponge is best eaten within a day. Being fatless, or containing little fat, it dries out very quickly. However this type of cake freezes well.
• Madeira (pound cake) and Victoria sandwich cakes will keep for up to 2 weeks in an airtight container.
• Rich fruit cake will keep for months. Leave the cake packed in the lining paper from baking. Overwrap in clean greaseproof paper* and pack in a polythene bag, plastic wrap, foil or an airtight container.

Quick Tip
Do not wrap fruit cake directly in foil. The acid content of the fruit will react with the foil, causing it to disintegrate in tiny particles on the surface of the cake.

CALYX CUTTER

Made of metal or plastic, in a variety of sizes and slightly different shapes. For use with sugarpaste* or pastillage*. Place a calyx on the back of a moulded* or cutter* flower while still soft. Alternatively, place the calyx in a greased mould and arrange the petals over it. The calyx supports the petals in the second method.

Quick Tip
As well as for cutting out a calyx for a flower, use the calyx cutter to cut out flowers. Mould a small piece of pastillage into a Mexican-hat shape, with a wide brim and tall, thin crown. Place the calyx cutter over the hat and cut out the paste. Model the centre to make a flower with five petals, using the thin crown as the base.

CANDLES

Even adults love to blow out candles! Look out for trick candles which will not blow out. The candles re-light after a few seconds and they can eventually be extinguished by snuffing them out.

Candles of equal height can be rather dull – particularly if there are a lot of them! They look more interesting if graduated in size, for example, placing the tallest in the middle of a cake and graduating the size down towards the side. To cut candles mark a line on each candle and cut with scissors.

Novelty Candles
Small animal-shaped candles for children's cakes. Number candles for adults as well as children, birthdays or anniversaries.

Attaching Candles to a Cake
• Pipe a rose in royal icing* on backing paper and place a candle through the centre.

- Mark a hole in sugarpaste* while the surface is soft, remove the candle and replace it when the cake is decorated.
- Use marshmallows as bases for candles. Heat a metal skewer and use it to bore a hole in each marshmallow.
- Use a skewer or fine-pointed knife to make a hole in a cork. Cover most of the cork with tiny flowers and position the candle in the hole.

CARBOXYMETHYL CELLULOSE

Known as CMC, this light-textured white powder is a synthetic cellulose which expands when wet. It is used to replace some or all of gum tragacanth* in pastillage* recipes. It is a cheaper alternative to gum tragacanth.

CELLOPHANE
See papers, coverings and wrappings.*

CHOCOLATE

A versatile ingredient available as either plain, milk or white chocolate. Confusion is sometimes caused by the many types. Here is a quick guide.

Dessert Chocolate: Manufactured for eating (and delicious) but difficult to work with if melting and using for cake decorating.

Cooking Chocolate: High-quality chocolate available from some good supermarkets, for example as Menier or own brands. Used for all forms of chocolate cookery, such as sauces, cakes and desserts but not easy to use for decorating purposes. This product has a good flavour.

Couverture: Good-quality chocolate, this needs to be tempered before use.

Chocolate-flavoured Cake Covering: Not a true chocolate, this contains vegetable fat to replace the cocoa butter. This is inexpensive, easy to use, it melts and sets well; however it does not have such a good flavour. Useful for everyday cakes or children's cakes but not for high-quality results.

Cocoa Butter

Fat present in the cocoa bean when it is harvested. The more cocoa butter in the chocolate product, the better it tastes but the less easily it will melt and set. Check the percentage of cocoa butter (or solids) on the label. Cake decorating shops sell a type of chocolate specially prepared for cake decorating. It has a balance of cocoa butter for flavour with added vegetable fat so it is easy to use.

Melting Chocolate

Chocolate melts at blood heat so little heat is required to soften it. Put the broken chocolate in a bowl over a saucepan of hot water, away from the heat source. Do not allow the base of the bowl to touch the water. Leave until melted. This will depend on the size of the pieces of chocolate and the amount in the bowl. Chocolate retains its shape as it melts and needs a gentle stir to become fluid.

Always wipe the base of the bowl when taking it away from the water. Do not allow any moisture to enter the bowl of chocolate as the two react to cause the chocolate to stiffen and separate slightly.

Microwave Method

Chocolate may be melted successfully in a microwave on low or defrost setting. The timing depends on the thickness of the chocolate and the amount. Check frequently: it is better to check every 30–50 seconds than to find separated or even scorched chocolate.

Quick Tip
Pour leftover melted chocolate into an airtight container. Cover when cool and store in the refrigerator. Re-melt as required.

Carob

The carob bean is taken from a tree grown in the Mediterranean area. Carob is processed into a chocolate-like substance but without the caffeine which is naturally present in the cocoa-bean. Ideal for migraine sufferers who avoid caffeine.

Available as dairy milk carob or in a variety of forms – for example as Easter eggs or bars with fruits and nuts. Soya bean carob is available for those allergic to dairy milk carob.

Chocolate Varnish
A tasteless varnish based on alcohol. Used to give a gloss to set chocolate. The smell which is evident when the container of varnish is opened dissipates on use.

Tempering Chocolate
Couverture chocolate contains different fats which melt at various temperatures. These need to be worked so that they set at the same temperature and in the form of small crystals. This gives the chocolate its gloss and 'snap' which is characteristic of expensive chocolates.

The chocolate is melted down to an exact degree, for which a chocolate thermometer is necessary. Pâtisserie chefs who are adept at this work test the temperature of chocolate on their lower lip which is particularly heat sensitive. Once melted, the chocolate must be cooled quickly, either by standing it over ice or by pouring it on a marble slab and using a palette knife to fold and spread it. It is then reheated to an exact degree for working. If the process is not carried out properly, the chocolate will not set well and the fat will separate, causing a film to spoil the gloss when set.

Common Faults in Chocolate Work
Fat Bloom: White surface on chocolate. Caused by the set surface melting slightly when left in over-warm conditions and setting again to leave a film of fat on the surface.
Sugar Bloom: When chocolate becomes damp some of its sugar content dissolves. When dried again the sugar crystals re-form into a larger pattern leaving a white bloom on the surface of the chocolate.

Chocolate Caraque
Pour melted chocolate on a flat surface and leave to set. Use a chef's knife to scrape off long, rolled curls of chocolate. Hold the knife at an acute angle, gripping the blade firmly with both hands. Leave the caraque in a cool place until using.

Chocolate Curls
Use a potato peeler to curl thin strips off the side of a block of chocolate. Dessert chocolate will need to be softened at room temperature for a few hours first. Place the curls in the refrigerator to firm up before use.

Chocolate Leaves

Wash and dry rose leaves with small stalks. Use a palette knife to spread melted chocolate on the back of the leaves and leave to dry. Apply a second coat. Hold the stalks, then peel the leaves away from the chocolate.

Chocolate Roses

Use just over half the weight of liquid glucose* (clear corn syrup) to melted couverture chocolate. Stir gently together and leave until set. If the chocolate mixture is too soft to mould, then re-melt it adding more melted chocolate. Mould the roses using the same technique as for moulded flowers*. If the paste becomes sticky, dust it with a little cocoa powder. To thin the petals place them inside a plastic bag. Delicately coloured chocolate flowers can be made by adding blossom tints* to white couverture chocolate. Keep your hands as cool as possible; holding them under cold running water and drying occasionally helps.

> **Quick Tip**
> *Weigh the jar of liquid glucose (clear corn syrup) without the lid. With the jar on the scales, use a hot, wet spoon to remove the required weight of glucose.*

Chocolate Shapes

Pour melted chocolate on non-stick paper* and quickly spread it out evenly to a depth of about 2.5 mm (⅛ in). If the paper shows through the chocolate, cover the patches with more melted chocolate. Chocolate contracts as it dries, so weight down the corners of the paper to keep it flat. When the chocolate is firm, but before it sets hard, cut it into squares, triangles and diamonds. Use a large, sharp knife to make long, neat cuts.

> **Secrets of Success**
> *For glossy shapes, use a shiny surface to set chocolate. Matt paper, such as greaseproof, does not give the chocolate a glossy finish.*

Piping Chocolate

Use a small paper piping bag. Add a few drops of glycerine to 30–60 g (1–2 oz/1–2 squares) melted chocolate. Stir gently until starting to stiffen. Place in the piping bag and cut a small hole in the tip of the bag. Start to pipe immediately. The chocolate has a limited working time before it starts to set.

Spinning Chocolate

Place melted chocolate in a small paper piping bag. Cut a tiny hole in the bag and quickly flick the bag back and forth over the top of a cake. Be sure to apply equal pressure on the bag as you work.

Uses for Spinning Chocolate

- Spin milk chocolate on a coat of dark chocolate.
- Spin chocolate across buttercream or whipped cream.
- Spin chocolate on small fancies.

> **Quick Tip**
> *If the chocolate stiffens in the piping bag, hold it against the side of a hot saucepan until melted again.*

COCOA PAINTING

A technique using cocoa powder combined with melted cocoa butter. The cocoa butter is melted and varying amounts of cocoa powder are added to obtain different shades of brown.

Uses

The cocoa mixture can be painted on sugarpaste*, pastillage* or marzipan*. The paste must be firm and dry before applying the decoration. A cream-coloured base, and varying shades of brown cocoa paint, are used to produce pictures resembling old sepia (a dye obtained from cuttle fish) photographs.

Mastering the Technique

Unless you are good at drawing it is better to trace the picture and mark it on the base. Keep the liquid warm. Use good quality brushes: a medium size for larger areas and a fine brush for painting thin lines. Start painting the background and the lighter shades first, adding the dark tones later.

Texture and highlights can be added by using a sharp knife to scrape away small areas once the cocoa paint has set.

> **Quick Tip**
> *If cocoa butter cannot be obtained use coconut oil or vegetable fat. Add petal dust instead of cocoa powder to create coloured paints.*

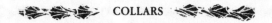

COLLARS

See also run outs*, for reference. An icing collar is a fragile royal icing* run out that extends beyond the edge of the cake. The most delicate collars have open sections within the run out, often part filled with piped designs. A collar will make a small cake look larger.

Types of Collars
One-piece collars completely surround the top of the cake. Collars which surround the base of the cake can also be placed on the board in two ways: by piping an outline on the board and flooding it or by making a separate collar and lowering it down over the cake until it sits on the board. The latter method calls for exact measurements and steady hands. Also, the side of the cake must be perfectly straight – if it slopes out at the base the collar will not fit.

Collars Made in Sections
Made in sections and positioned around the top edge of the cake, this is an easier method than making a complete collar. Remember that each iced section will usually be slightly bigger than the paper template and allow for this when working out the design. It is better to leave a small space between each section of collar than to find that the finished collars will not fit around the cake.

Double Collars
Two collars of equal size, one positioned above the other and supported by means of hidden stars of royal icing.

Floating Collars
Two collars one above the other, supported by very fine lines of icing piped close together. The bottom collar is positioned on the cake and small supports are placed at regular intervals on top of it. The top collar is lowered to rest on the supports, then lines of piping are worked from the top collar down to the bottom collar in sections. Once a section of piping is dry, the support is removed. A space is left when piping to remove the last support when all the icing is dry, then the space is completed. These collars are extremely fragile. It is most important that the supports are all exactly the same depth.

Templates

Take exact measurements when the cake has been iced. Allow for the collar to extend 5 mm (¼ in) over the top surface of the cake. Ensure that the collar will not protrude over the board.

Papers

Use smooth waxed paper*. Cut a 2.5 cm (1 in) slit in the centre of the paper when making a circular run out to allow for the paper shrinking. Non-stick paper* is suitable for small collar sections. Smooth cellophane* is easy to remove and clear.

Perspex

Ideally, collars ought to be piped on perspex or glass. These surfaces are rigid, flat and attract warmth which encourages the collars to dry.

Piping

Use a small bag and a fine writing tube (tip) for piping the outline.

Flooding

Thin royal icing with egg white. Bang the bowl of icing on the working surface to bring air bubbles to the surface. Break the bubbles by drawing a knife across the surface of the icing. Leave the icing to stand for 15 minutes, covered with a damp cloth, then repeat the process of banging and pricking bubbles. You will need a large piping bag of icing to flood a large collar. If the design has inserts, a small bag will help to flood the icing into narrow sections.

Have the flooding icing ready in the piping bag before starting to pipe the outline. Once the outline is piped, immediately cut a hole in the bag and start flooding. The size of hole should correspond to the size of the run out. Do not make the hole too large or the icing will flow out too quickly, also air bubbles will flow through large holes. The hole should be about the size of a no. 2–3 icing tube (tip).

The tip of the bag should be kept down in the icing as the surface is flooded to expel air bubbles.

On a large collar, do not work in one direction only, otherwise the edge of the flooding icing will be dry before you completely flood the collar. Work for short distances in clockwise and anti-clockwise directions alternately until the whole area is flooded and smooth. This way there will not be any indication of where the icing started to flow.

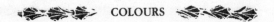

Drying

Position a lamp with a flexible arm over the collar at a height of about 15 cm (6 in) to dry the surface and give the icing a gloss. Leave the collar to dry in a warm room, or in the airing cupboard, supporting the base on blocks to allow the warmth to circulate.

Applying the Collar to a Cake

To remove the paper from a large collar, place it near the edge of a table and gently peel the paper down, turning the collar around gradually.

Alternatively, turn the collar upside down on a level surface and peel away the paper a little at a time.

Use a star tube (tip) and stiff royal icing to pipe a rope inside the top edge of the cake. Gently lower the collar into position and leave to set before moving the cake.

Quick Tip
To repair a small area of broken collar, stick a piece of plastic bag, slightly larger than the break, on the underside of the collar. Repair with icing and leave to dry, then peel away the plastic.

COLOURS

The wide range of edible colours available originates from the three basic colours: red, blue and yellow.

Liquid Colours

Easy to mix, these blend well into liquid icing, such as glacé icing*, or buttercream*. However, the colours are not concentrated and they can soften paste icing excessively. It then requires more icing (confectioner's) sugar to restore the consistency and this, in turn, lightens the colour.

The bottles are easily knocked over, so look out for the type with a dropper.

Uses

For royal icing* and glacé icing or buttercream. Liquid colours may be used to tint royal icing but if a strong colour is required for piping the liquid colour will spoil the texture of the icing, making it too thin to pipe.

Liquids will give an even blend of colour to flooding icing. Stir the colour into the icing very gently. To remove colour from a bottle use either an eye dropper, obtainable from the chemist, or the tip of a cocktail stick.

Remember . . .
Cochineal is pink not red. When it is in the bottle it may look red, however it will not give a red colour.

Paste Colours
Easy to use and concentrated so only a small amount is needed. Ideal when deep colours are needed and for painting. Care must be taken to blend the colour into the icing to avoid producing streaks.

Uses
For royal icing, marzipan*, sugarpaste*, glacé icing and buttercream.

Powder Colours
Referred to in this book as blossom tints, also known as petal dust. Fine powders in a wide range of colours. See blossom tints*.

Uses
For dusting on flowers, frills and pictures to give a delicate effect. Powders may also be used to colour royal icing: an expensive method, best used when colouring a small quantity of icing to pipe decorations to match a dusted area. For instance, to colour piped roses to match a garrett frill* which is dusted with colour.

Care must be taken when using the powders as they tend to float in the air and land at random on the surface of the cake.

Gold and Silver Lustre Colours
Edible powders with added sparkle. These can be moistened to use for painting but only for delicate shades as they do not give a great depth of colour.

Gold and Silver Colours
Non-toxic paint for use on plaques* and non-edible items. The paint settles at the base of the bottle and needs to be stirred well before use.

Chalk Colours
Ordinary children's colouring chalks, they are non-toxic sticks of colour available from art shops. Scrape a fine powder off the chalks and use for dusting on non-edible decorations.

Colour Wheel

Obtainable from art shops, this device is designed to help understand how to mix colours. For example, the colour wheel shows red as the opposite colour to green so by adding red to green it will dull the colour.

Colouring Sugarpaste*, Pastillage* and Marzipan*

Add the colour with a cocktail stick. Knead the colour into the paste until it is evenly distributed. Cut the paste in half to check that the colour is even.

 Quick Tip
Label the top of each jar of colour, then they can be identified at a glance.

Colour Combinations

Experiment by mixing colours to discover the many effects that can be achieved. Not only is this fascinating but it is an excellent way of producing life-like colours, unusual shades and delicate tints. Here are a few useful basic combinations. Vary the ratio of one colour to another to make quite different shades.

Red + blue	= purple
Blue + yellow	= green
Red + yellow	= orange

COOKING FOIL
See papers, coverings and wrappings.*

CONFECTIONERY GLAZE

A clear, edible glaze which may be used on plaques*, flowers or other work. The same as chocolate glaze* but lighter in colour, this protects finished work from moisture as well as making it look attractive.

CORNELLI WORK

Also known as scribbling and 'take a line for a walk', a description borrowed from the art world. Cornelli work is not a haphazard

Left: the correct method of piping cornelli work. **Right:** lines should not be short and broken as they look unattractive.

technique of piping lines but a tightly controlled design which gives a delicate appearance.

> **Quick Tip**
> *Cornelli work is useful for hiding small cracks in royal icing* and flaws in sugarpaste*.*

Piping

Use royal icing in a small piping bag fitted with a fine writing tube (tip). Hold the tube (tip) at a 45° angle either touching, or very close to, the surface. Pipe the icing to resemble the shapes of jigsaw pieces, with no sharp angles, in a close pattern of curves, near to each other but not touching. The joins must be invisible and a fine, damp, paint brush should be used to eliminate any unwanted ends of icing.

Uses

- To decorate a cake board.
- Piped on the exterior of pastillage* bells.
- As part of a design on a cake or plaque*.

COUVERTURE
See Chocolate*.

CORN SYRUP

American term for liquid glucose*. Also known as clear corn syrup.

CRAFT KNIFE

Small, sharp knife, similar to a scalpel, available from cake decorating shops, this is useful for cutting out paste. One type has two removable blades: a small blade for intricate work and a straight-topped blade for ribbon insertion.

Most kitchen knives are either too large to handle for delicate work or not sharp enough to cut the paste without dragging it.

CREAM

For filling and decorating cakes, usually gâteaux*. Two types of cream can be whipped: whipping cream and double (heavy) cream.

Whipping Cream: Contains 35% butterfat and is pale, almost white, when whipped. Whipping cream takes longer to whip than double (heavy) cream because it contains less fat. It does not give as firm a consistency and it does not hold its shape as well as double (heavy) cream.

Double (Heavy) Cream: Contains 48% butterfat and is cream coloured. Double (heavy) cream whips up very quickly, it is firmer and it holds its shape longer than whipping cream. It very soon curdles and becomes buttery if overbeaten.

Whipping Cream – Creating Volume
An 18th century cookery writer wrote of 'flogging cream until stiff', a term with broader general use in those days but not the way to treat cream!

Chill the cream, bowl and whisk. A hand (balloon or spiral) whisk gives the greatest volume but involves hard work. A rotary whisk or hand-held electric beater are quicker. Do not use a very large electric beater as it is easy to overwhip cream in such a machine. Use a bowl large enough to hold four times the amount of unwhipped cream. This will provide plenty of space for whipping air into the cream. The cream is ready for piping when it is *just* holding its shape in peaks. Do not overwhip the cream or it will have a slightly rough, almost curdled, appearance when piped. The process of spooning the cream into the piping bag and squeezing it out tends to stiffen it slightly, particularly in warm weather.

Piping Bags

Paper bags are not suitable as they very soon become soft from the moisture of the cream. A nylon piping bag may be used but some fat or liquid tends to ooze out through the fabric, making it wet and unpleasant to hold. A cloth bag that can be boiled is the best for piping cream.

Icing Tube (Tip)

Use a large star icing tube (tip). If the opening in the tube (tip) is too small, the cream will separate.

Filling the Piping Bag

Place the tube (tip) end of the piping bag in a wide-topped jug and extend the bag over the edge of the jug, down around the outside. This will make it easier to fill the bag by spooning in the cream. Twist the top of the bag to stop the cream from coming out.

Using Whipped Cream

Pipe on fatless sponges, genoese sponge or chocolate cakes. Mark a covering of cream by swirling it with a pointed knife or smoothing into even 'waves' with a large palette knife.

Keeping Qualities

Cakes decorated with whipped cream should be eaten on the same day as prepared. Cream turns yellow if left and it can pick up flavours from other foods. Store in the refrigerator.

Freezing

Whipped cream freezes well for up to 4 months, in a rigid covered container.

> **Quick Tip**
> *Line a baking sheet with foil. Pipe rosettes of cream on the tray and open freeze until firm. Pack carefully in a rigid container. To use, simply place the rosettes directly on the cake and leave in the refrigerator for a couple of hours or in a cool room until softened.*

Frozen Cream

Double (heavy) and whipping cream are available ready frozen, unwhipped. Packed in small chunks or sticks, this is a great standby, also economical, as only a small amount need be thawed as required. For best results thaw the cream in a covered container in the refrigerator, a few hours ahead or the day before using. For quicker thawing leave the sticks at room temperature or speed the process by placing in the microwave for about 10 seconds on a medium or low setting. Do not heat the cream as it tends to separate, becoming unsuitable for whipping.

CREME AU BEURRE

Also known as boiled buttercream and continental buttercream. Boiled sugar syrup is whisked into egg yolks, then softened butter is gradually beaten in. A delicious buttercream that should be made with care but the effort is worthwhile. A smooth cream that can be used to fill, coat and pipe on cakes. Keep the syrup away from the beater when pouring it on the eggs. Soften the butter well and add it a small amount at a time.

Temperature Test

This test also applies when making American frosting*. For making crème au beurre the sugar syrup must boil to 107°c (225°F). This is known as the thread stage. A sugar thermometer is helpful but not essential. Test the sugar syrup by dipping a wooden spoon into it as it boils. Use your forefinger and thumb to remove some syrup from the edge of the spoon. Press your finger and thumb together, then separate them. A thread of sugar should form if the correct temperature is reached and the syrup boiled sufficiently.

Secrets of Success
When the syrup has boiled sufficiently, dip the base of the saucepan into cold water to prevent the syrup from over-cooking.

Problem Solving

If the mixture curdles, place the bowl over a pan of warm water and stir until the crème au beurre is smooth again.

Uses

As a filling and covering for light cakes, for example fatless sponges, all-in-one cakes and Victoria sandwich cakes.

CRIMPERS

Metal implements obtainable in a variety of designs and used to pinch together soft sugarpaste* to make a pattern. Crimping is a quick and easy way to decorate sugarpaste-covered cakes. Some crimpers have a rubber band around their bases to ensure they do not spring open too wide when in use.

Practise on a small piece of paste. Remember to crimp the paste when the cake is freshly coated or the paste will crack.

Using

To ensure complete control, hold the crimpers near to their serrated edge. Use even pressure when pinching the design into the paste. If the crimper sticks in the paste, dip it into cornflour (cornstarch) or icing (confectioner's) sugar before using, or wash and dry it well. Release the tension gently from the crimper. Do not allow the crimper to open fully in the paste or it will stretch, and spoil, the pattern.

A very effective design can be made – even on wedding cakes – by crimping a pattern around the sides of a cake. Heart or holly designs can be crimped and the design coloured.

Piping

The crimped designs can be overpiped with royal icing* either in the same colour or in a contrasting colour.

Uses

- Around the edges of plaques*.
- As a frame for a picture in icing.
- Around the top and sides of a cake.
- As a border for ribbon insertion*.
- Around the edge of a sugarpaste covering on a cake board.

CRYSTALLIZED FLOWERS

A quick and unusual decoration, crystallized flowers are edible, depending on the type of bloom used. Delicate coloured crystallized flowers make an ideal decoration for a Mother's Day cake.

Choose small flowers with smooth petals: primroses, violets, the blossom from fruit trees or rose petals and mint leaves. Leave a small stalk on the flower for ease of handling.

Preparation

Colour small amounts of caster sugar the same colour as the flowers. Place the sugar in a plastic bag, add the colour and rub the bag between your hands to distribute the colour evenly. Pour out on a plate and leave to dry.

Secrets of Success

Petal dust may be used to colour the sugar. You will need a stand to hold the flowers while they are drying. Cover a cup, or basin depending on the number of flowers, with a circle of greaseproof paper*, secure it down around the side with a rubber band.

Gum Arabic Solution

Place 10 ml (2 teaspoons) rose water in a cup with 5 ml (1 teaspoon) gum arabic*. Stand the cup in hot water until the gum dissolves, stirring occasionally. Leave to cool.

The flowers must be absolutely fresh and perfect, clean and dry. Using a medium paint brush, lightly coat the whole of the flower with the solution. Sprinkle a thin layer of sugar all over the flower. Pierce a hole in the paper stand to support the flower. Leave to dry in a warm dry room, away from moisture. The flowers are brittle once crystallized and they attract moisture from the atmosphere if kept in a humid place.

Keeping Qualities

Store the crystallized flowers between layers of tissue paper in a warm dry place. Do not cover with an airtight lid as they tend to soften. They keep for a few weeks, depending on the type of flowers.

CURTAIN WORK

The term used for fine lines of piping which are part of extension work*. They extend from the side of the cake to the built out bridge work*. They are piped in royal icing* using a small bag fitted with a fine plain writing tube (tip).

Mark the top guideline for the design using a sharp tool: the fine groove is useful when beginning the piped lines of icing, as it provides a 'grip' for attaching them to the side of the cake.

Piping

The lines should be piped as close together as possible. Dabbing the opening of the icing tube (tip) on a damp sponge between piping lines can assist in attaching the icing on the cake. This keeps the opening clean and the icing slightly moist.

Place an object under the back of the cake board to lift it slightly and tilt the cake forward. This will ensure that the piped lines hang vertically rather than sagging inwards. Pipe each line past the base of the bridge work and neaten the excess end with a fine damp brush before the icing dries. It helps to work with the cake at eye level, even if this means kneeling down. Be careful when turning the cake, the wet iced lines can stick together.

Board

The board must be strong and at least 7.5 cm (3 in) larger than the iced cake to protect the piping. A light board can cause the work to shatter through vibration or flexing.

Designs

The top edge of the curtain work may be a straight line, a scalloped edge or pointed edge. Heart and bell shapes may also be used. When the curtain work is dry, staggered tiny dots of icing may be piped on the lines. Pieces of deep lace can be made separately and attached to the bridge work.

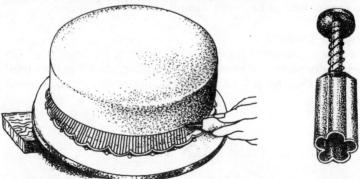

Left: piping curtain work.
Right: a plunger cutter for stamping out cutter flowers.

Secrets of Success
The longer the lines of piping, or the deeper the curtain, the more difficult the work. Practise the technique on small, short examples of the design.

CURVED FORMER

A piece of plastic which looks like a pipe cut in half lengthways. Also available with a double curve. A curved former is used to hold decorations in a curved position while they are drying. Decorations can be dried inside the former or over the back of the curve. A rolling pin, bottle or cardboard roll can be used but remember to check that the curve is not too acute and that the object is firmly supported in a stable position.

CUTTER FLOWERS

*Flower Paste**
Pastillage*, petal powder* or flower paste should be firm and pliable so that it can be rolled until transparent without tearing. The most life-like flowers are made from paste that is so thin that you can read through it. Finger nails need to be short for this work or they can mark the soft paste. When working with the flower paste try to keep the amount of cornflour (corn starch) or icing (confectioner's) sugar to the minimum. Cornflour (corn starch) will dry paste out quicker than icing (confectioner's) sugar but it is much finer to use.

Cutters
Made in metal, nickel silver and plastic. They should have sharp cutting edges and they must not buckle when pressed. Alternatively, it is possible to use cardboard templates and to cut around the edge to make petals and leaves from flower paste; however, the edge will not be as sharply defined and the paste may drag when cut with a knife.

Quick Tip
The piece of circular plastic with some cutters is to prevent the cutter's edge from marking the hands.

Flowers on Wires

The petals are cut, then modelled around a wire. If possible use fresh flowers in season as a guide or, as good substitutes, use a book of botanical flower paintings or a gardening catalogue. Keep at least one of each variety of the finished flowers for future reference.

To give large roses extra strength, use a piece of 24 gauge wire and push it up through the centre of the cone of paste. Hook the end of the wire and moisten it, then pull it back down into the paste. This ensures that the hook catches in the paste. Finish moulding the rest of the flower.

Flowers without Wires

Grease a cocktail stick (toothpick) with white vegetable fat. Cut out the petals and model them around the stick. Leave until completely dry. Carefully remove the flower from the stick.

Stamens

The finer the stamens, the more authentic the flowers look. The easiest way to fix the stamens is to tape them on the end of floral wire, making sure they are at slightly varying lengths, then arrange the petals around them. Or they may be placed into the centre of the flower when it has been made, before it dries.

Secrets of Success

If the stems of the stamens are soft, dip them into confectionery glaze*, then leave to dry and harden. They will be far easier to use.

Colouring

Petals may be dusted with colour when they are cut out and before modelling or once they are wired and dry.

Use a good-quality paint brush and load the powder on it from a flat surface. To highlight the petals, draw the brush just over the edge of each petal from the back of the petal forward to leave a glow of colour along the edge.

Blend silver dust in with a colour to give extra sparkle. Matt, white stamens can be coloured with food colourings.

Problem Solving – Dry Paste

Rather than adding extra egg white or water which will make the paste sticky, add a small amount of white vegetable fat to lubricate the paste.

DESIGN

The best-executed decorating techniques can be spoilt by badly planned designs. Thought should be given to the overall design before the cake, or cakes, are baked, particularly when working with tiered cakes.

Plan
Draw up an accurate plan. Designs can be made larger or smaller by scaling them on graph paper; however, an easier method is to have an enlarged or reduced photocopy taken of the design. This is an inexpensive service available in local print shops or other outlets with suitable photocopiers.

Proportions
Cakes should be made in proportion: small cakes should not be too deep, large cakes should not be very shallow. A band of ribbon or a deep base border can help to break the height of a cake, making it appear less deep. Wide, shallow cakes may need an upstanding border around the top edge to compensate for the lack of height.

Texture
Create interest by combining smooth and textured surfaces. For example, the smoothness of a sugarpaste-covered cake combined with an area of the design piped in cornelli work*; stippling royal icing with a natural sponge will give a textured surface and this technique is both quick and easy to apply.

Spacing Decorations
Allow space for all piping and decorations so that the attention is focused rather than being drawn in many different directions. An evenly spaced, repeated pattern creates harmony. A spray of flowers of numerous shapes is not as effective as one made from three or four types of blooms. For inspiration look at the arrangements in a florist's shop. A name or message on a cake

should have plenty of space around to ensure it commands maximum importance.

Using Colour
By repeating colour you can link up different types of decoration used on a cake. Always repeat a colour somewhere on a cake, even in a different shade, or perhaps by reflecting the colour of the icing in a ribbon.

Unless you are making a novelty cake, do not use too many colours as this can become distrac

Cake Stand
Contributes to the overall impression of the cake. The stand should repeat the shape of the cake and its depth must be in proportion to the bottom tier of the cake.

Spiral Metal Stand: A stand of this type adds space and movement to the display of a wedding cake. The metal curves can be eye catching and create a hard impression. Decorated discreetly with flowers and ribbons to complement the cake, this type of stand provides an attractive modern surround.

DUMMIES

Used as a base on which to practise piping and designing decorations.

Wood: Available round and square, also in some other basic shapes, these are heavy and stable with a large base. May be ordered from specialist cake decorating shops. Expensive but worthwhile for serious practising. Moisten with water to remove hardened icing.

Polystyrene: These are lightweight and inexpensive. Available in a variety of shapes and sizes to use for practising piping techniques and for working out designs. Use an all-purpose craft glue or royal icing to stick the dummy on a heavy base. Without careful handling, the polystyrene can crumble away when icing is removed.

> **Quick Tip**
> *Cover a polystyrene dummy in a coat of royal icing to protect the surface.*

EGGS

Should be fresh and obtained from a reputable source. Store eggs in their covered cartons in the refrigerator and take the required number out some hours before cake making. Discard any eggs with cracked shells.

> **Quick Tip**
> *When cracking eggs, use a teaspoon to remove any pieces of shell that may drop into the bowl.*

Whisking Egg Whites

Use a perfectly clean, glazed earthenware or stainless steel bowl and scald it with boiling water. Dry well with a clean tea-towel or absorbent kitchen paper. Plastic bowls can retain grease on their surface so are not suitable.

Egg whites will not aerate if any grease is present. The smallest amount of grease breaks down the bubbles in the whites, preventing them from trapping, and holding, air. The whites become fluffy and white when whisked due to air being trapped in their structure.

Freezing

Reconstituted dried egg white and fresh whites can be frozen. Allow sufficient room in the container for the liquid to expand. When required, thaw out in the refrigerator. Whites may be stored for up to 6 months.

Egg yolks may be frozen separately but they must be combined with a small amount of sugar and they do not keep as well as whites. They should be used within 1–2 months.

ELECTRIC BEATER

Also known as a food mixer. A heavy-duty electric beater, of the type with an integral stand and optional attachments, is a great asset to a cake decorator. This type of machine may be used for mixing stiff batches of rich fruit cake* and for beating royal icing*. It is also useful for whisking the lightest of sponges and for making large quantities of buttercream*.

A hand-held machine is suitable for many tasks but it will not cope with the heavy mixes, when the motor could be burnt out if the machine is overloaded. A hand-held beater is more suitable for whipping cream. If you do whip large quantities of cream in a larger machine, take care not to overwhip it.

Royal Icing*

When made in a machine this can very easily be overbeaten. Use the beater attachment rather than a whisk implement which will rapidly turn the icing into a fluffy meringue-like mass. Keep the machine on the lowest speed and add the icing (confectioner's) sugar gradually until the mixture is of a soft peak consistency. The longer the icing is beaten the whiter it will be.

> **Remember . . .**
> *Always check the manufacturer's instruction book to ensure that the machine is suitable for mixing the quantity which you are preparing.*

EMBOSSED SILVER OR GOLD PAPER
See papers, coverings and wrappings.*

EMBOSSERS

Small implements with a relief design on their surfaces, used to stamp a pattern into soft sugarpaste* or pastillage*. The design may be coloured by painting with food colour or petal dust.

The process probably evolved from the embossing tools used to create designs on leather work. This is a quick and easy method of applying patterns to a sugarpaste surface. Mark the pattern while the paste is still soft. Apply only enough pressure to stamp the design and avoid making a mark with the base, or edge, of the embosser.

An easy way of embossing the top of a cake is to use a stiff plastic doiley. Place it on top of the soft sugarpaste. Start in the centre of the cake and use a rolling pin to roll towards the back.

Start again in the centre and roll forward. If anyone is available, ask them to hold the doiley firmly while the design is rolled on. Depending on the type of cake, a firm cake board can be placed over the doiley and pressed down evenly.

Quick Tip
Look out for buttons, badges or other firm items which have a raised pattern on their surface and are suitable for marking a shape into sugarpaste or pastillage. Thoroughly wash and dry them before use, using a new hard toothbrush to clean the tiny areas in the raised pattern.

EQUIPMENT

Buy as you need and gradually build up a comprehensive stock. Specially designed sugarcraft boxes have plenty of compartments to hold equipment; however, a fishing tackle box is equally efficient and often less expensive. These boxes are easy to carry and they have individual sections to hold equipment. Here are a few of the many items that are useful and which make life easier for a cake decorator.

Cranked Artist's Palette Knife: Useful for sliding under run outs* or to pick up lace pieces. Make sure it is rustproof.

Desk Lamp with Flexible Arm: For drying run outs*.

Electric Beater or Food Mixer:* Invaluable for beating large quantities of cake mixture. Also useful for the following.
• Whisking egg whites.
• Beating sponge batters.
• Making royal icing* in quantity.
• Making buttercream* in quantity.
• Blending colour into sugarpaste*.

Icing Tubes (Tips):* Remember that different manufacturers produce different sizes. The best quality are precision made from nickel silver and they appear to be seamless. The seam in the metal is visible in icing tubes (tips) of lesser quality.

Long White Plastic Rolling Pin: To enable a large piece of paste to be rolled out without leaving marks. Keep wrapped in polythene especially for rolling sugarpaste.

Long Serrated Knife: To cut through gâteaux* easily.

Metal Rule or Icing Ruler:* Sometimes called a straight edge. To smooth royal icing. A plastic ruler will bend.

Modelling Tools*: The bone-shaped tool is one of the more versatile of these.

Non-stick Board: Keep especially for flower modelling.

Paint Brushes: Use a 2.5 cm (1 in) brush to apply apricot glaze* to cakes. This is easier than using a pastry brush. You also need a good-quality fine brush for delicate work.

Palette Knife: With firm blade, 10–15 cm (4–6 in) long. Make sure the blade is rustproof. A long-bladed table knife with a rounded end makes a good substitute.

Brush Tube (Tip) Cleaner: To clean out icing tubes (tips).

Scrapers: For smoothing royal icing or buttercream on the sides of cakes. Made of plastic or polished stainless steel, these are available with many different edges to give a variety of finishes. Plain and serrated or comb edges are the most common; however, others include scallop and dot patterns.

A plain edge with one notch may be used to mark an even, continuous ridge around a cake. This provides a useful guide for adding decoration, for example when applying loops. Triangular scrapers combine two or more different edges.

Quick Tip
Move a serrated scraper up and down slightly as you work to mark a pattern of wavy ridges.

Small Nylon Sieve: Kept especially for making icing.

Smoother*: To achieve a smooth surface on sugarpaste*.

Spacers or Marzipan Spacers: To roll out marzipan to an equal thickness. The spacers are used underneath the rolling pin, placed on either side of the paste which is being rolled. This ensures that equal pressure is applied all over the paste. Without spacers, if unequal pressure is used the result is an uneven surface.

Turntable*: Must turn easily (check before buying) and be a suitable height.

Wallpaper Brush: To brush the work surface free of icing (confectioner's) sugar and cake crumbs before washing down.

Wooden Spoons: Kept especially for beating royal icing.

EXTENSION WORK

A built-out design consisting of bridge work* and curtain work*. The extension work extends from the base of a cake. This is a technique for the experienced decorator, skilled at using fine icing tubes (tips) and with a steady hand.

Bridge Work*
This is piped around the base of the cake, built up by overpiping line upon line, usually in a scallop design. The number of lines of piping will depend upon the size of the tube (tip) used. These lines are left to dry.

Curtain Work
Fine lines piped to drop vertically from the side of the cake out to the edge of the bridge work. These lines should be spaced so closely that not another line can be piped between them; however they must not be joined together.

Secrets of Success
Start the first line of piping in the middle of each scallop, or section, and work outwards on either side. This method ensures the lines do not gradually go off at an angle.

Colour
The base covering on the cake may be brushed with a pastel blossom tint* before the extension work is applied. This will glow through the work. Alternatively, the bridge work may be piped in a contrasting colour or the curtain work may be coloured. Tiny dots, known as hail spotting, piped on the curtain work may be worked in a contrasting colour.

Secrets of Success
Use blossom tint to colour the icing for piping. Most paste colours contain glycerine which would weaken the lines of curtaining or bridge work.

Designs
The top edge of extension work can be shaped to create interest, rather than working from a straight edge. Several rows of extension work may be applied in tiers to the side of a cake. Extension work can be applied in small sections, it does not have to form a continuous band around the cake. For example, heart shapes may be worked at intervals around the base of a cake.

Fluted Extension
The bridge work is built out with each row being slightly shorter than the last. This gives an attractive horizontal curve to the extension as it flows around the base of the cake.

FEATHER ICING

Also known as marble icing. This technique adds a professional finish to glacé-iced cakes.

Colours
Colour the icing for piping slightly deeper than required as it tends to weaken on being dragged through the soft base icing. This is one cake decorating technique which looks good using a bright colour because the lines of colour are very thin. A design using two colours is also very attractive.

Preparation
Have ready the cake brushed with apricot glaze*, the glacé icing* ready over heat or the royal icing* of a flooding consistency. Have small piping bags filled with coloured icing; scissors and a fine-bladed knife, fine metal skewer or cocktail stick (toothpick) for dragging the icing.

Icing
Most usually worked in glacé icing but royal icing can be used very successfully on more sophisticated cakes. The icing for piping does not need to be as fluid as the surface coating.

Technique
Flood the cake with the icing. Use a palette knife to carefully encourage the icing outwards but try to let the icing flood of its own accord. If the icing does not flood satisfactorily, place the cake on a wire rack, then tap the rack up and down to move the icing.

Cut a small hole in the piping bag filled with coloured icing 'and pipe lines across the flooded icing. Quickly draw the back of a knife, fine metal skewer or cocktail stick (toothpick) across the lines. Wipe the implement clean after each stroke.

> **Quick Tip**
> *Before attempting this design on a cake, have fun experimenting on biscuits (cookies). Use plain tea*

> *biscuits (cookies), that will not crumble easily. Once
> iced, place them in the oven on a very low heat,
> with the door ajar. Remove when the icing is firm
> and they will be crisp to eat on cooling.*

Use

Use glacé icing on fatless sponges, Victoria sandwich, Madeira-type cakes (pound cakes) and small fancies. Use royal icing on fruit cakes.

FILIGREE
See cornelli work*.

FLOWER NAIL

Also known as an icing nail. A circular piece of plastic or metal attached to the top of a long nail-like holder. Most flower nails have a flat top but some may be slightly domed.

Use

To support flat flowers while they are being piped. A square piece of non-stick* or waxed* paper is placed on the flower nail, held in place by a dab of icing. The flower is piped on top of the paper which is then removed and the flower left to dry. The flower nail is held in one hand and the flower piped with the other. The nail is rotated as the flower is piped.

Icing Tube (Tip)

A petal tube (tip) is used to pipe a variety of flat-based flowers, such as daisies, violets, pansies and primroses.

> **Quick Tip**
> *As an alternative to a bought flower nail, spear a
> cork on top of a cocktail stick.*

FLOWER PASTE

Used primarily for hand-modelled flowers, this can also be used for other decorations.

There are various recipes for making the paste, which should include gum tragacanth*. This gum strengthens the paste and enables it to be rolled out until it is translucent. Flower paste can be home made or bought from the cake decorating suppliers, either in small blocks or as petal powder*, ready to mix with water.

Home-made Flower Paste

Use a heavy-duty electric beater. The stiff consistency of flower paste needs a strong beater. Sprinkle the gelatine over cold water and leave for about 15 minutes to 'sponge' before placing over a saucepan of hot water to dissolve.

Liquid glucose* used in the paste is stiff when cold but once warmed it becomes fluid. Remove the glucose from the jar with a hot, wet spoon. Scrape away any excess liquid glucose that is attached to the base of the spoon. Remember that the quantity should be measured using standard measuring spoons.

When adding the egg white, keep part back and only add it if needed.

> **Secrets of Success**
> *Once the paste is made, leave it for at least 24 hours before using. This allows the gum tragacanth to swell and gives the paste its full stretching power.*

Keeping Qualities

Store the paste tightly wrapped in a plastic bag inside an airtight container in the bottom of the refrigerator. The paste will keep for weeks but because it contains gelatine, which is an animal product, it will eventually produce tiny spots of mould.

Freezing

Can be frozen in small blocks. Wrap well in polythene, freeze, then place in an airtight container for longer storage. Allow to thaw overnight in the refrigerator before use.

FLOWERS

See Blossom Cutter*, Briar Roses*, Buttercream Roses*, Chocolate Roses, Crystallized Flowers*, Cutter Flowers*, Ganache*, Moulded Flowers*, Piped Flowers* and Pulled Flowers*.

FONDANT

Available from some specialist cake decorating shops in the form of a firm white paste. Can also be bought as a powder to which either water or fruit juice is added.

True fondant, not to be confused with sugarpaste*, is softened over heat and flooded on cakes. The bought fondant is inexpensive and usually superior to any made at home.

Making Fondant
Fondant is made by boiling sugar syrup to 115°c (240°F). A small amount of liquid glucose* or cream of tartar is added to stop the liquid crystallizing. When the correct temperature is reached the liquid is cooled quickly and agitated, or worked, to form small sugar crystals. This may be done on a marble slab using a palette knife to 'fold' the syrup. The mixture gradually thickens then it is kneaded until smooth before being stored for future use.

Flavouring
When the fondant has melted, add grated chocolate, coffee essence or essential oils – use only a drop or two as they are very strong. Essential oils are available from health food shops. Stir until the flavouring is evenly mixed: chocolate should be melted into the fondant before use.

Colouring Fondant
To obtain a variety of colours from one batch of fondant, use the following method. Start off with white, then add yellow. Next add pink to obtain peach, then add green. Finally, add brown colouring or cocoa powder to obtain a brown icing. The colours may be used separately on individual cakes or to create a design, for example feather icing may be worked in fondant.

To Use
Place the fondant in a bowl over a saucepan of hot water, away from the heat, until melted. Stir until lukewarm to the touch. If overheated the fondant will lose its gloss. If the fondant is too stiff, stir in a little prepared sugar syrup.

Quick Tip
Run water over the surface of the fondant to help it soften before melting. Literally hold the lump of fondant under the cold tap for a few seconds.

Preparing the Cake

If the fondant is poured directly on the surface of the cake it will lose its gloss as some will be absorbed by the cake. To prevent this, apply a thin coat of marzipan* to the cake surface. Alternatively, brush the cake with hot apricot glaze* and allow it to cool before coating with fondant.

Coating a Cake

Stand the cake on a wire rack placed over a baking sheet. Leave plenty of space between individual cakes. For small cakes use a wire rack with a small mesh to prevent the cakes from overturning. Pour the melted fondant into a hot wet jug and carefully pour it over the cake.

Versatility

• For a smooth, buttercream-type icing, warm fondant then beat in half its weight of unsalted butter.

• Softened fondant with added icing (confectioner's) sugar and peppermint oil may be kneaded and used to make peppermint creams. Roll out to 5 mm (¼ in) thick, cut out shapes and leave until firm. The peppermint creams may be half dipped in melted chocolate.

• Pipe melted, flavoured fondant into chocolate shells. Leave to crust over, then top with more melted chocolate to seal in the filling in home-made chocolates.

• While hot, fondant may be used to stick flowers to the side of a cake which is coated in royal icing* or sugarpaste. Dip the base of the flowers in the hot fondant, then apply them to the cake – particularly useful when arranging cascades of flowers down the side of a wedding cake. This is the *only* way in which the fondant is used hot and it may be helpful in other situations as an 'edible glue'.

GANACHE

A mixture of chocolate and cream which has a variety of uses. Single (light), whipping or double (heavy) cream may be used.

Proportions

Use double the amount of chocolate to cream, for example 250 g (8 oz/8 squares) chocolate to 125 ml (4 fl oz/½ cup) cream. Bring the cream to the boil in a small saucepan. Melt the chocolate and add the cream, then whisk both ingredients together. If necessary the mixture can be re-melted by warming it in a basin over hot water.

Quick Tip
Block chocolate may be grated into the warm cream. The higher the quality of the chocolate the better the gloss on the ganache.

Use

• While the ganache is liquid, flood it over a gâteau*.

• Whisk while the ganache is warm and beginning to set, until lighter in colour and creamy. The ganache should hold its shape and it may be piped at this stage.

• Leave to set to a firm paste, then cut into shapes to use as centres for dipped chocolates.

• Whipped as for piping, then rolled into balls and coated in cocoa powder or grated chocolate this makes truffles – useful for decorating a simple chocolate gâteau.

• Ganache may be used in the same way as buttercream*.

Ganache Roses

Beat the ganache until it holds its shape. Use a large petal tube (tip) and medium piping bag, then pipe roses, see piped flowers*. For a larger rose, pipe the ganache around a piece of thin dowelling which has been shaped to a point at the end. Leave the roses until firm before use.

Freezing Ganache Roses
Piped and moulded roses may be frozen for up to 2 months. Place in the refrigerator the day before using.

GARRETT FRILL

A frill of sugarpaste*, named after a South African lady, Elaine Garrett, who introduced the idea. Frills can be applied in a straight line along the base of a cake, in scallops around the sides of the cake and in overlapping layers. The frill can also be applied around the top edge of a cake and made to stand out; it may be used to surround a plaque*, or it may even be attached upside down by inverting the cake to apply the frill. The frill should be allowed to stiffen before turning the cake the right side up.

Template
It is important to make an accurate template to fit the area of the cake. Mark a fine groove into the icing on the cake along the top of the template to show where to attach the frill.

Secrets of Success
The cake needs to have deep sides to show off a scalloped frill to perfection. If the cake is too shallow, apply a straight frill around the base.

Cutters
Special garrett frill cutters are available from cake decorating shops. A scone cutter or a straight length of paste may also be used. If the centre of the circle has to be cut out, remember that the smaller the section cut out of the middle, the deeper the frill.

Pastes
Sugarpaste is most often used to make frills. However a mixture of one-third flower paste* to two-thirds sugarpaste will result in a stiffer paste which will hold its shape well. A deep frill is heavy and it may well need the additional support given by combining flower paste and sugarpaste.

Frilling the Paste
Start by brushing a thin line of water along the template line on the cake. This will make the paste slightly sticky and help to make the frill adhere.

Use a wooden cocktail stick (toothpick) as plastic will not grip sufficiently. Roll out the paste to approximately 2.5 mm (⅛ in) thick, or slightly less. If the paste is too thick it will not frill.

The paste dries out quickly, so cut one section at a time. Roll along the edge of the frill with the cocktail stick (toothpick), using firm pressure. If the paste splits, discard the cocktail stick (toothpick) for a new one – it may have become impregnated with sugar. Carefully cut the circle across and straighten it out.

Secrets of Success
If the paste splits along the top edge, try frilling the paste before cutting out the centre portion of the paste. This way, the edge of the paste does not dry out.

Attaching the Frill
Brush a second line of water to the section of cake required. Support the frill on the palm of the hand, then gently and quickly stick it on the moistened cake.

Chocolate Frills
Make the chocolate paste as for chocolate* roses. This paste can be rolled out thinly and cut to make garrett frills. If the paste is sticky, use a little cocoa powder when rolling out. Use the end of a paint brush to frill the edge of the paste and attach it to the cake with melted chocolate.

Two types of garrett frill cutters.
Left: one-size round cutter with scalloped edge. **Right:** scalloped cutter with removable centre sections for making frills of different widths.

Decoration

If the frill is applied to a freshly coated cake, crimpers can be used to join the frill to the sugarpaste on the cake. The frill is much thinner to crimp than the surface of the cake, so be sure to apply most of the crimped design to the cake surface.

Broderie Anglaise Decoration: May be added by stamping a pattern of holes before attaching the frill. Do not make too many holes or the frill will weaken. When the frill has dried, pipe outlines around the holes in royal icing* using a fine writing tube (tip).

Royal Iced Cakes

Frills can be applied to royal icing. Pipe a line of icing just below the marked line on the cake, then press the frill, firmly but gently, in place.

> **Secrets of Success**
> *Support the frill on a piece of thin card as you attach it. A quick method of decorating the top edge of the frill, and also making sure it is well applied, is to run a dressmaker's tracing wheel along the edge while the paste is still soft. The rounded end of a small paint brush may also be used to mark decorative impressions in the edge of the paste.*

Flouncing the Frill

One method of lifting the frill is to pipe a rope of royal icing fractionally below the marked line on the side of the cake. Apply the frill when the icing is dry and it will flow over the iced line.

While the frill is soft it may be lifted. Run a paint brush sideways under the frill to lift it slightly. Position cocktail sticks (toothpicks) at intervals into the cake to support the frill. Leave until the frill is dry, then carefully withdraw the sticks. Alternatively, place rolls of plastic wrap under the frills and remove them with tweezers when the frill is dry.

Double Frill

Apply a frill around the cake. Leave to dry. Position a second frill, overlapping the first by about half its depth. A third frill can be applied if desired. Layered frills are always applied from the base upwards.

Colouring

The cut-out paste can be dusted with colouring before the frilling

technique is applied. This way the blossom tint* can be brushed on directly where it is required. Frilling the paste will ensure the dust clings into the paste. This method also reduces the risk of breaking the frill, which may happen if brushed once the paste is on the cake and dry.

However, to obtain a coloured edge only on a frill, dust it with colour once it is dry. Load a paint brush with colour and apply the tint from underneath the frill. This will coat the edge of the frill with blossom tint.

Quick Tip
When applying layered frills, make each layer of frill a paler shade than the last one.

GATEAUX

The French word for cakes, generally used in culinary terms for highly decorated, light cakes based on sponges and often completely covered with a soft cream mixture.

A base of fatless sponge, Genoese sponge or Victoria sandwich is sliced into layers and sandwiched with one or more fillings. The layers of cake are often moistened with liqueur or a flavoured stock syrup (sugar dissolved in water, brought to the boil, cooled and used as required). The decoration may be simple – a dusting of icing (confectioner's) sugar – or more elaborate with toppings such as chocolate, whipped cream, crème au beurre* or buttercream*.

Preparation
Cut a small groove down the side of the cake. This will help in placing the layers of the cake back in the same position. Lay the palm of the hand flat on top of the cake and use a serrated knife to cut the layers.

Portion Control
When the gâteau has been coated but before adding the decoration, mark the top of the gâteau into equal portions.

Torten Divider
A rigid, circular plastic divider with blades radiating from the centre. Used to divide a gâteau into portions of exactly the same size.

Types of Icing for Gâteaux
Lemon or orange curd, jams, whipped cream, ganache*, chocolate buttercream, fondant* and buttercream*.

Decorations
Piped decorations, chopped nuts, fresh fruit, chocolate shapes, feather icing*, vermicelli and marzipan*.

Quick Tip
Return the gloss to dull vermicelli, by placing in a basin over hot water for a few minutes.

GELATINE

A substance extracted from protein found in bones. Available in two forms, powdered, which is the most common, and leaf.

Powdered Gelatine
Always add gelatine to the liquid, not the other way round. Sprinkle it over cold water, do not stir, and leave to stand for 15 minutes. By then the gelatine will have absorbed the water and swollen to a spongy consistency. This process is known as sponging. Stand the bowl over hot water, away from the heat, and leave, without stirring, until the gelatine has dissolved completely into a clear liquid. Stir before use.

Leaf Gelatine
Sheets of clear, brittle gelatine, embossed with a diamond pattern, available from specialist shops.
Dissolving: Place the sheets in a bowl of cold water and leave to soak for 10 minutes. If the pieces of gelatine are too large, they can be broken into smaller sections; however, do not break them into small pieces. By this time the gelatine will be soft. Remove it from the liquid and dissolve it in the required amount of liquid, in a bowl over hot water, away from the heat.

Quick Tip
When using leaf gelatine, 4 sheets, 23 × 7.5 cm (9 × 3 in) weighing 15 g (½ oz), will set 625 ml (1 pint/ 2½ cups) liquid. When using powdered gelatine, 15 g (½ oz/3 teaspoons) will set the same volume of liquid.

Decoration

Leaf gelatine may be used to make very realistic lattice windows for models. The diamond pattern, already imprinted on the gelatine, creates the authentic look. The size of the pattern may need to be reduced, in which case use the tip of a red hot wire to score extra lines on the leaf gelatine – it will not melt. Attach the windows to the model with royal icing*. A stained-glass window effect can be made either on the windows of a model or on the surface of a cake. This effect is achieved by placing a drawn design under the gelatine and tracing it, using food colour and a paint brush, straight on the gelatine. Do not have too much liquid on the paint brush when painting the sections.

GLACE ICING

Quickly made and applied, this is a liquid icing for flooding over cakes and biscuits. It dries very quickly.

Ingredients

Water and icing (confectioner's) sugar give a semi-transparent coating. To obtain a more opaque finish replace the water with egg white. This results in a whiter icing and one which will allow time for adding decorations before it starts to dry out.

Preparation

If possible coat the base of the cake as this is usually a firmer, flatter surface. Brush with hot apricot glaze* and leave to cool before coating. The glaze creates a barrier and stops the icing sinking into the cake surface.

Consistency

Although this icing is quick to make it can cause trouble when it is too thin, in which case it will run off the cake, or too thick, when it will not flow. Stir the icing gently. Do not beat it or air bubbles will appear and they are difficult to remove.

Test for Consistency: Think of a puddle and raindrops. Drop just a little of the icing from a teaspoon into the bowl of icing. The impression made by the drop should disappear after a moment or two. For a large cake use slightly thinner icing than for small cakes.

Flavouring

Replace the water with orange or lemon juice for tangy flavour to complement the sweetness. Add coffee essence or dissolved cocoa powder. Other flavourings may be added as wished.

Coating the Top and Side of a Cake

Put the cake on a wire rack over a baking sheet. Pour all the icing over when the apricot glaze is dry. Immediately tap the rack on the work surface to tease the icing all around the side of the cake.

> **Remember . . .**
> *Place any decorations on the icing before it dries or it will crack.*

GLYCERINE

Sweet, colourless and odourless liquid, also known as glycerol, which attracts moisture from the atmosphere.

Use

In cakes to delay the staling process. In paste colours and piping gel* to keep them moist. Glycerine is also added to royal icing* to prevent it setting too hard.

GREASEPROOF PAPER
See papers, coverings and wrappings.*

GUM ARABIC

A pale-coloured powder obtained from an acacia tree. Gum arabic is available from specialist cake decorating suppliers. To dissolve the gum completely, place it in a small basin. Add cold water, then stir and stand the basin over hot water until the gum dissolves.

Use

• As a hot glaze on petits fours once removed from the oven.
• As a glaze applied to dry marzipan animals or fruits.
• As an edible glue, for example to stick the petals of small pastillage* flowers together.

GUM PASTE

There are many recipes, containing either gelatine* or gum tragacanth* to make a stiff white paste. This is used for making models, such as churches, containers and decorations for the tops of cakes. The paste dries out quickly when exposed to the air and should be stored in a tightly closed plastic bag, then placed in an airtight container.

Use

Cut off a piece of paste and knead it until it is soft enough to work with. A small amount of vegetable fat can be worked into the paste if it cracks. Gum paste is not suitable for making flowers.
Models: Place the rolled-out paste on a flat-surface, preferably glass or perspex. Use a long, sharp knife to cut out pieces. Do not drag the knife or make small cuts. Cut out any other sections, without moving the paste. Leave to dry in a warm place without removing from the glass. Turn over after 24 hours.

Quick Tip
When making models, sand down the edges of the pieces before joining them together.

GUM TRAGACANTH

A gum extracted from a small tree or bush found in Mediterranean countries, including Greece and Turkey; Iran and Syria. The name is derived from *tragakantha* – *tragos* (goat) and *akantha* (thorn).

It is available as a cream-coloured powder which expands when moistened. It is expensive but only a small amount is needed to stiffen paste.

ICINGS

This chart shows which icings to use on different cakes.

	ROYAL ICING	SUGARPASTE	GLACE ICING	BUTTERCREAM	CREME AU BEURRE	AMERICAN FROSTING	MELTED CHOCOLATE	WHIPPED CREAM
RICH FRUIT CAKE	•	•						
LIGHT FRUIT CAKE	•	•						
MADEIRA CAKE		•	•	•		•	•	
VICTORIA SANDWICH		•	•	•	•	•	•	•
ONE-STAGE CAKE		•	•	•	•	•	•	•
CHOCOLATE CAKE		•	•	•	•	•	•	•
GENOESE SPONGE		•	•	•	•	•	•	•
FATLESS SPONGE			•	•	•	•	•	•

ICING TUBES (TIPS)

Buy the best quality icing tubes (tips) from specialist cake decorating suppliers. These are made from nickel silver and they have virtually invisible seams. The best icing tubes (tips) have well-defined points and sharp definition to any serrations. They should be long and narrow to fit perfectly into a paper piping bag without leaving a gap for icing to ooze out. Price is always a good guide to quality. Cheaper icing tubes (tips) are sometimes badly seamed which may result in the icing twisting as it flows out.

Sizes
All icing tubes (tips) have numbers stamped on them but the sizes indicated by number vary from one manufacturer to another. The cheaper quality writing tubes (tips) have larger openings.

Screw-on Tubes (Tips)
These are intended for use with screw adaptors and nylon piping bags. The bags are too big and difficult to grip for fine work.

Icing Syringe
Difficult to use and far too large for most work. It is not easy to control the amount of icing pushed out from these gadgets.

Savoy Tubes
Made in cream-coloured plastic as well as metal, with plain or star design. Used to pipe quantities of whipped cream, these are fitted in a heavy-duty material piping bag.

Care of Icing Tubes (Tips)
Soak the tubes (tips) immediately after use in a cup or basin of water. A fine brush cleaner is useful to clean the opening. Do not poke a sharp implement into the point as this could damage the edge. Always check that the hole at the end of a fine tube (tip) is clear before drying and storing.

Storing Tubes (Tips)
Store separately to avoid damage. Plastic boxes can be purchased with individual compartments to house the icing tubes (tips).

Suggested Uses for Popular Icing Tubes (Tips)
No. 1 Writing: Lines, trellis*, filigree*, writing, dots and loops*.
No. 2 Writing: Lines, trellis, writing, dots and loops.
No. 8 Star: For buttercream* and royal icing* shells and stars.
No. 12 Star: For buttercream stars, shells and rosettes.
No. 43 Star: For royal icing stars and shells.
No. 44 Star: For royal icing stars, shells and scrolls.
No. 22 Basket Work: For royal icing basket work*.
No. 57, 58, 59 Petal: Different sizes of petal tubes (tips) for making a variety of flowers and frills. Also for left-handed users.
No. 59 Large Petal: For piping buttercream or ganache* roses.

KNIVES

The choice and quality of knives is all important. The right knife can make all the difference between success and failure.

Cook's Knife: A heavy kitchen knife with a long, straight blade. This is used to cut a straight edge in one movement. Useful for marzipan* and sugarpaste*.

Craft Knife: A small, scalpel-like implement with a sharp, wedge-shaped blade. For making small cuts in modelling work. To slit petals on pulled flowers and other fine cutting operations.

Cranked Palette Knife: With an extra thin blade, obtainable from art shops. Some may not be rustproof, so check before buying. This thin and flexible blade is useful for sliding under run outs* and lace* sections.

Long Serrated Knife: For slicing gâteaux* and levelling the tops of cakes.

Palette Knives: Stainless steel with firm blades, 15 cm (6 in) and 10 cm (4 in) blades. For spreading buttercream* and royal icing*.

Wedding Knife

The bride and groom make the first cut into the wedding cake using the ceremonial knife which may have a pearl handle. A cluster of small flowers and ribbons may be tied around the handle. A regimental sword may be used in place of the knife. Once the cake is taken behind the scenes, a large, sharp, cook's knife should be used for cutting it into pieces.

LACE WORK

An old needlecraft skill which has been copied in icing and applied to modern cakes. The lace is piped in separate pieces using royal icing*. Once dry, the pieces of lace are attached to the iced cake with dots of icing.

Template
With practice, lace may be piped freehand; until then use a template of the lace pattern. Graph paper, marked with coloured lines to denote the required depth of the lace, is a half-way alternative to a template.

> **Quick Tip**
> *Draw a row of the lace pattern pieces, each slightly apart to allow for piping. Attach a tag of stiff card to the bottom of the sheet of paper: use this tag to slide the paper as you finish piping each row of lace pieces.*

Icing
The royal icing should be made with egg white or pure albumen powder*. If the icing has been made using an electric beater, beat a small amount with a wooden spoon for a few minutes to achieve a smooth texture. The icing is best made a day ahead to allow it to settle.

> **Secrets of Success**
> *To eliminate air bubbles, and any minute grains of hard sugar, force the icing through a piece of nylon stocking. Keep a piece of new stocking in your cake decorating kit for this purpose, scalding it before and after use to keep it perfectly clean. This is one of the finest sieves available and it is ideal for any fine work.*

Piping

The size of the icing tube (tip) will vary according to expertise: the more experienced you are, the finer the size. However, do not use a tube (tip) larger than no. 1. Experiment with piping on a sloping surface similar to a draughtsman's board – some cake decorators find this an easier way to work.

A design without too many joins is quicker to work and it looks neater. If the top of the lace is pointed, place the template with the point facing towards you. Pipe one side of the piece of lace, ending at the point. Then pipe the second side, bringing the line of icing to finish at the point and to complete the section of lace.

Choice of Paper

As well as wax paper*, pipe the lace on teflon-coated paper*, smooth roasting wrap* or cellophane*. When dry, the lace pieces may be removed easily from all these types.

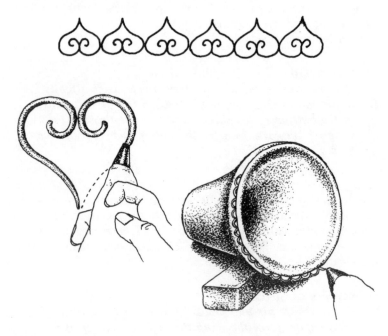

Top: a typical, simple lace pattern which may be used as a template.
Left: pipe down to the point of the lace.
Right: piping hanging loops on a bell instead of attaching lace sections.

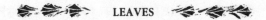

Attaching the Lace to the Cake

Pipe a small section of icing along the line on the cake. Attach the lace while the icing is still soft. Alternatively, pipe two dots of icing on a piece of lace, then apply it to the cake.

Quick Tip
Attach a sheet of lace design templates on a firm board and use as a permanent fixture for immediate use.

Short Cuts

Lace can be tedious to make so it is worth taking a few short cuts when you are familiar with the technique.

Square Cake: Pipe a horizontal line on the paper. While the line is wet, pipe lace pieces which touch both the line and each other. Once dry, attach the lace to the cake in strips.

Bell: A quick way of attaching lace around the edge of a moulded bell – place the bell on paper and draw around the outside edge. Draw a second line 5 mm (¼ in) inside the first line. Use the inside line as a template to make small lace pieces, all touching each other. Once dry, turn the lace over carefully. Pipe a line of royal icing around the edge of the bell and place it gently on top of the lace circle.

Alternatively, support the bell sideways and pipe hanging loops on a section of the edge. Allow to dry before moving the bell to pipe another section.

Colouring Lace

Use blossom tints* to colour the icing for lace. Most paste colours contain glycerine* which attracts moisture from the atmosphere and they will soften the lace.

LATTICE
See trellis.

LEAVES

It is important to match the leaves with the flowers for best effect on a cake. Some leaves which grow naturally with their flowers are not necessarily the best choice for use on the comparatively small cake surface – tiny lily of the valley flowers and their large

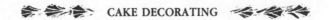

leaves are a good example. Also, a contrasting leaf can look wonderful, as in the case of roses displayed with variegated ivy leaves.

> **Remember . . .**
> *Always curve leaves as you make them so that they dry into a realistic shape.*

Leaf Cutters

These are available in too many shapes and sizes to list, from rose or ivy leaves to oak and holly leaves.

Marzipan* and Sugarpaste* Leaves

As well as using leaf cutters, diamond shapes may be cut and marked with the back of a knife, for example to make holly leaves.

Rose Leaves

Press the back of a clean rose leaf on thinly rolled paste. Use a cocktail stick (toothpick) to pull out tiny points around the edge of the leaves. Do this by making a tiny scratching movement at the edge of the paste.

Piped Leaves

A leaf piping tube (tip) may be used. Alternatively place firm buttercream* or royal icing* in a strong piping bag. Push the icing down to the point of the bag. Using the thumb and forefinger, flatten the point of the bag horizontally, then cut an arrowhead shape in it. Keep both sides of the arrowhead equal in length. The buttercream or icing can then be piped directly on the surface of the cake.

Pastillage Leaves
Make these using a cutter and mark them with a plastic veiner.

Wired Pastillage Leaves
Burn the paper coating off the top 1 cm (½ in) of the wire. Moisten the end of the wire and place it in the leaf. This gives a neater result as the paper covering on the wire tends to show.

Chocolate Leaves
See chocolate*.

Bought Leaves
Available in green, gold or silver paper, with or without wires. Silk and satin leaves are sold as well as the old favourite dried fern.

LIQUID GLUCOSE

Known as corn syrup, or clear corn syrup, in America, glucose is a simple sugar. Liquid glucose has a thick, syrupy texture and it becomes runny when warmed. Obtainable from cake decorating suppliers and chemist shops.

Quick Tip
Chemists also sell powdered glucose – this is chemically pure glucose which is not the same as liquid glucose.

Use
• Liquid glucose attracts moisture and it is used in a variety of pastes to keep them pliable.
• Add a small amount of liquid glucose to a sugar syrup to prevent crystallization.

LOOPS

Are a graceful addition to the side of a decorated cake. If a cake is too deep, pipe two or three layers of loops to give the impression that the cake is less high. They look very authentic on a drum novelty cake, particularly if piped in red.

Marking the Cake

Mark the cake before piping the border along the top edge. Use a template to mark sections measuring about 3.5 cm (1 ½ in). The wider and deeper the loops are made, the more difficult it is to pipe them and to control their shape.

Piping

Use a small bag with a writing tube (tip). The icing should be well beaten and it should flow easily out of the tube using a small amount of pressure. Have the cake positioned at eye level and with the top tilting slightly away from you.

Touch the icing tube (tip) to the cake surface to connect the icing. Then draw the icing away, keeping up the pressure on the bag, and let it hang before touching the icing tube (tip) back against the cake to attach the icing. Do not try to pipe against the side of the cake. Allowing the loop to hang will let it fall into a natural curve.

Secrets of Success

Counting as you pipe each loop of icing helps to achieve an even rhythm and therefore an equal length for all the loops. To make a large loop, start from the top edge and allow the thread of icing to flow down to the centre of the loop. Start the second half of the loop from the opposite top edge then secure the thread of icing in the centre. Disguise the join in the centre of the loop with a suitable decoration.

Upturned Loops or Arches

Use a firm support with a diameter smaller than the cake, for example a smaller cake tin, and cover it with a clean tea-towel. Place the cake upside down on the support. Pipe the loops hanging down and leave to dry before carefully turning the cake upright.

MADEIRA CAKE

A plain cake similar to American pound cake, this may be used as an alternative to Victoria sandwich when a firm surface is required for decorating. To lighten the texture of the cake, slice through it twice and sandwich together with a filling such as flavoured buttercream*.

Madeira cake may also be used as an alternative to a rich fruit cake* for a celebration cake. Marzipan* and royal icing* or sugarpaste* can be used to cover the cake.

Crinoline Lady Cake

The shape of this cake requires it to be cooked in an ovenproof basin or bowl, or a Dolly Varden tin, the name given to a tin formed in a basin shape. Because of the depth of the cake a Victoria sandwich mixture tends to sink, therefore the firmer consistency of Madeira cake is ideal for the longer cooking time required.

Quick Tip
Madeira cake differs from Victoria sandwich cake in the proportion of flour to other ingredients, it contains more flour to fat. This makes it more stable for making larger, deep cakes which may sink if made with Victoria sandwich mixture.

MARZIPAN

Has been around for a long time – the oldest recipe said to be in existence dates from the 1400's and was written of as 'massepain' in a French recipe devised by nuns.

Home-made Marzipan
Can be made with whole egg, egg yolk or the whites alone. The

last does not have as much flavour but it keeps for longer. The large amount of sugar used acts to some extent as a preservative but if made with egg yolk alone, it is best to use the marzipan within a few days.

Secrets of Success
Do not overwork the marzipan by kneading it for too long as the oil will be released from the almonds making the paste greasy. A recipe which involves making a sugar syrup, then adding ground almonds and egg will always be smoother than one made by mixing all the ingredients together.

Bought Marzipan or Almond Paste
If the word marzipan or almond is used on the packet this indicates that the product is made up of about two-thirds almonds and one-third sugar.

The pale marzipan is of higher quality than the yellow variety.

Powdered Marzipan
A ready-to-mix marzipan available from some specialist cake decorating suppliers. Cooled, boiled water is added and mixed to a paste. This product may then be used as for ordinary marzipan.

This powder keeps well and is useful when a small amount of marzipan is needed. It can be made up as necessary and saves having spare packets of marzipan which may harden.

Remember . . .
When adding the water, do not add the total quantity at once: too much will make the marzipan sticky and by adding additional icing (confectioner's) sugar you will spoil the proportions in the mix.

Applying Marzipan to Cakes
Roll out the marzipan between spacers to ensure that it is evenly thick. Use a long, sharp knife to cut a straight edge in one movement. Roll out marzipan on icing (confectioner's) sugar, not flour or cornflour (corn starch) which could ferment if trapped between the cake and marzipan. When rolling marzipan keep it moving to stop it from sticking to the work surface.

Always apply marzipan to the base of the cake and use that for the top surface.

Covering the Side of the Cake

When applying apricot glaze* to the side of the cake, ensure that it does not spread too near the marzipan on the top. If any glaze smudges on top of the marzipan it can cause a stain to show through on royal icing*.

Roll out a long sausage shape of marzipan by hand, then flatten it. Use a rolling pin to roll the marzipan to the required thickness, then cut it to the depth and circumference of the cake. Roll up the paste like a bandage and wrap it around the side of the cake, overlapping the cut edges.

Secrets of Success
To obtain a neat join, make a clean vertical cut through the two layers of overlapping marzipan and remove the surplus.

Applying Marzipan for Sugarpaste* Covering

If the cake is deep it can be difficult to remove the pleats that form in the marzipan. Therefore apply the marzipan separately to the top and sides and use the palm of the hand or a plastic smoother to blend the top edge of the cake into a soft curve. Leave to dry for 3–4 days, covered loosely with greaseproof paper.

Keeping Qualities

Marzipan will dry out if exposed to the air. Wrap it well in a plastic bag to keep it soft and pliable, then store in a cool, dry place. If the marzipan has become hard, warm it for a few minutes to make it softer.

Design Idea
A top decoration of marzipan needs a textured surface to make it interesting. This can be achieved by rolling with an embossed rolling pin, by pressing a plastic doiley into the surface or by marking the marzipan with crimpers. A short length of scrubbed, new, ribbed garden hose may be used to roll an impression into the marzipan.

MARZIPAN FLOWERS

See moulded flowers*. Marzipan is an excellent medium for modelling flowers. It is pliable, easily coloured, soft enough to model yet stiff enough to hold its shape. A variety of flowers can be modelled by hand, including roses, daffodils, fuschias and carnations.

Storing
Leave the flowers to dry in the air. Store in a cardboard box, supported by tissue paper.

METAL RULE

Also known as a ruler, royal icing blade or straight edge. A metal rule will hold its shape when smoothing the icing across a cake surface. The edge should be fine and smooth, without any indents or flaws that may mark the icing.

A ruler, rather than a knife, will obtain a smooth, flat coat of royal icing. The edge of a wooden ruler is too thick and a plastic ruler will bend with the weight of the royal icing.

MEXICAN PASTE

Traditional Mexican celebration cakes are often decorated with models of figures. The paste used for the models and their clothes is made from a combination of icing (confectioner's) sugar, gum tragacanth*, liquid glucose* (clear corn syrup) and water. Once made, the paste should be stored for a few days to allow the gum to expand, then it may be rolled out until transparent, cut to shape and used to 'dress' the models.

Secrets of Success
If the paste dries out, add a small amount of white vegetable fat or mix in some sugarpaste.*

MODELLING TOOLS

An invaluable help for modelling flowers, for marzipan* work and for many other uses, these may be purchased singly or in sets.
Pointed Piece of Wooden Dowelling: For making pulled flowers*.
Bone-shaped Tool: This has two sizes of ball for marking eye

sockets, curving petals, making open mouths or thinning petals of small flowers.

Large Ball-shaped Tool: For thinning edges and cupping large petals.

Shell-shaped Tool: Used to mark feet or to press a design on sugarpaste*.

Thin-bladed Tool: Used to cut small sections of marzipan or sugarpaste and to make creases in marzipan fruits.

Cone-shaped Tool: Used for modelling trumpet-shaped flowers.

Serrated Cone-shaped Tool: Used for marking flower petals and marzipan fruits.

MONOGRAMS

Two or three letters linked together. This type of decoration is suitable for a wedding cake, using the initials of the bride and groom. It may also be used for highlighting an individual's initials, or those of a company, on a wide variety of celebration cakes.

Spacing
If the monogram is to be placed on the side of the cake, ensure there is also sufficient space for the top and bottom decorations. The monogram needs to have space above, below and around it to give it impact.

Use clear, simply curved lettering for monograms. Intricate detail can be hard to decipher.

Linking Initials
If possible, the initials should be interwoven two or three times,

such as: under, over, then under again. Some letters are more difficult to link, noticeably those composed of straight lines.

Trace the chosen letters on separate pieces of greaseproof paper* or tracing paper*. Place one tracing on top of the other and adjust the position of the letters until a well-balanced design is achieved. Allow space between the sections of the letters to ensure each one is readable. Trace this design on one piece of paper. For a clear guide when piping, colour the letters individually in bright colours.

Piping
The flooding consistency icing should be put in a bag and set aside. A small hole is cut in its tip just before use. Use a no. 0 or 1 writing tube (tip). Outline the monogram, then flood alternate sections. Leave each section to dry until the top surface of the icing has crusted over. Flood in the empty sections of the letters and leave to dry in a warm place.

> **Secrets of Success**
> *A desk lamp with a flexible arm can be used to dry the sections of icing. Position the lamp approximately 15 cm (6 in) away from the icing.*

Colouring Monograms
The icing may be coloured before piping or colour may be painted on once the monogram is dry. Gold or silver is often used for monograms but the paint used, although non toxic, is not edible.

Round Cakes
A monogram placed on the side of a round cake needs to follow the curve of the cake. Use a cake tin the same diameter as the cake and secure the template in position on it with dots of icing on the side of the tin. Support the tin on its side and pipe the monogram. A desk lamp with a flexible arm should be positioned immediately above the monogram to dry the top surface of the icing before it has a chance to move on the curved surface.

MOULDED FLOWERS

Roses are the most popular moulded flowers; others include carnations, daffodils and fuschias. Once you have mastered the technique of moulding roses you can progress to others.

Marzipan Roses

Marzipan is pliable and easy to mould so these are the easiest to make. Always keep the marzipan covered when working to prevent it drying and cracking.

Use the best-quality marzipan for modelling as cheap marzipan will crack when moulded. White marzipan is obtainable from cake decorating suppliers and some supermarkets.

Tips on Technique

• Make the petals about the same size in depth as in width – if they are too deep they will flop over.

• To create a curve at the base of the rose, thin the top half of the petal but keep the base thicker.

• Only make sufficient petals for each layer, then add them to the flower. Freshly moulded petals should stick to each other; if necessary apply a spot of water to the base of the petals.

• Curl back the petals as each layer is applied. A few cracks along the top edge can look quite authentic but not too many.

• As each petal is placed in position, press the base firmly together but leave the top free to curl back.

Colouring Roses

Colour is generally worked into the marzipan before modelling. Paste colours will not make the marzipan sticky. The easiest way is to thoroughly knead the colour into the marzipan on the work surface. If the paste is streaky the roses will be variegated.

Often, real roses are a deeper colour in the centre than on the tip of the petals. Colour a portion of paste dark for moulding the central petals, then gradually knead in extra uncoloured paste to mould outer layers of paler petals.

Sugarpaste Roses

Sugarpaste* is soft and experience is needed to successfully model flowers from it. The paste may be stiffened by adding ½ teaspoon gum tragacanth* to 125 g (4 oz/¼ lb) of sugarpaste. Leave the paste overnight, well wrapped, for the gum to expand. Use the same technique as for moulding marzipan.

Secrets of Success

If the paste becomes sticky, thin the petals inside a smooth plastic bag, then leave the flowers to dry with some support to keep their shape.

Attach the roses to the cake with royal icing or use a little sugarpaste mixed with water.*

NON-STICK PAPER
See papers, coverings and wrappings*.

NOVELTY CAKES

The description covers a wide range of shapes and designs, from a bottle of Champagne to a runway complete with aeroplane. Tins can be bought or hired for many designs, alternatively shapes may be cut out of a slab of cake; however, this quite often results in a lot of leftover cake. Work out the quantity of mixture required for tins of unusual shapes following the guidelines given for baking tins*.

Choice of Icing
Most novelty cakes are made from Victoria sandwich or Madeira cake (pound cake) and eaten within a few days.
Sugarpaste*: The usual covering for unusual-shaped cakes; however, the paste can be too sweet for some tastes. Roll out the paste just thick enough to make a smooth surface but not excessively thick.
Buttercream* Coating: Spread the surface of the cake with a thin layer of buttercream, then leave this to firm up in the refrigerator. Apply a second coat and decorate.

Covering Unusual-shaped Cakes with Sugarpaste
Follow the instructions under the entry on sugarpaste for covering the side of the cake with a sharp top edge. To cover the top of a cake, dust a cake board slightly larger than the cake with icing (confectioner's) sugar. Roll out the sugarpaste for the top of the cake and place it on the cake board, top surface down. Place the cake, upside down, on the sugarpaste. Cut away the surplus paste around the shape of the cake and place a board on the base of the cake. Holding both boards together, turn the cake the right way up. Remove the top board and neaten the edge of the paste.

Horseshoe Cakes: If the cake is coated in royal icing*, it can be difficult to ice within the curve of the horseshoe. Coat this area with a layer of sugarpaste in a matching colour, using a straight-sided jar to smooth the paste in place.

Character Cakes: Outline the facial details with piped lines of a deep colour. Fill in the remaining surface with piped stars of buttercream or royal icing.

NUMBER CAKES

A base of Madeira cake* (pound cake) or rich fruit cake* will give a firm foundation for decorating, in either a formal or comparatively simple style. Number-shaped tins or frames may be purchased or hired. Alternatively, a standard-shaped cake may be trimmed to represent numerals.

Number Templates to Cut Cakes
Measure the size of the tin in which the cake was baked and use graph paper to work out the measurements for the numerals. Transfer the design to thin card. To avoid unnecessary waste, make round cakes for round numerals, for example 0, 3 and 8; and square or slab cake for the remaining numbers.

Cutting the Cake
Use a knife with a long, straight edge to make a straight cut in one movement. A sharp, long but fine-bladed knife is best for cutting curves. If the cut edges of the cake crumble, apply hot apricot glaze* to set the crumbs or soft buttercream*. Place the cake in the refrigerator to firm the coating before applying the top coat.

Double Number Cakes
These need a large board of approximately 41 cm (16 in) to give sufficient space for displaying both cakes. Transfer iced cakes to the board one at a time: place the left hand cake on the board, then decorate its side and base. Sift icing (confectioner's) sugar on a piece of non-stick paper. Place the second cake on the paper and proceed to pipe the left hand bottom border and any side decoration on that side. Carefully lift the cake from the paper and slide it gently on the board. Continue with the rest of the decoration.

ORCHIDS

There are many varieties to copy as there are literally thousands of species. Flower paste* may be rolled out until transparent to model the petals. What appears to be a flower head made up of petals, in an orchid also includes sepals. Cutters can be bought for making some of the popular orchids. Here are a few of the better known types; consult a specialist, well-illustrated book for details.

Cataleya Orchid: A pretty flower with frilled petals.

Cymbidium Orchid: A large bloom with smooth petals and a well-marked tongue.

Phalaenopsis Orchid: Also known as a moth orchid due to its flat petals on either side.

Singapore Orchid: A small orchid often used in bridal bouquets.

Slipper Orchid: A name derived from the large pouch in front of the orchid.

Orchids can be made in two ways. Firstly, by cutting out petals and sticking them together immediately, in which case place small pieces of plastic wrap between the petals until they are dry to help give the flower movement.

Alternatively, wired orchids take longer to make but they are very realistic and the flower can be arranged once the petals are made. Each shaped petal has a wire threaded through the middle. Once the petals are dry the orchid is taped together.

Secrets of Success
Have a bowl of sifted cornflour (corn starch) ready. To curve the 'tongue', partly wrap it around a wide piece of dowelling. Place the tongue into the cornflour (corn starch), then carefully withdraw the dowelling, leaving the tongue upright and allow the front to curve down slightly.

Colour
A quick and effective way of colouring the mottled tongue is to use a toothbrush dipped into liquid food colouring. Use the

forefinger to gently pull back the bristles and release a fine spray of colour. The colour may be applied when the tongue is cut out and before shaping.

The bitter lemon colour gives a fluorescent glow to orchids.

OVERPIPING

Is a technique that needs a steady hand and considerable practice using fine tubes (tips). The lines of icing are built up one upon another, each line thinner than the last. The light and shade effect created gives a sculptured look. This is known as the English look or Nirvana style, which translates as 'the highest state of perfection'.

Three, Two, One
A common term is 3, 2, 1, used to describe step-like overpiping. The work starts with a line piped using a no. 3 tube (tip), then it is overpiped using a no. 2 tube (tip). Next, using the same nozzle, a line is piped alongside, very close to, the overpiped line. Then a no. 1 tube (tip) is used to pipe a line on top of the first

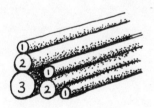

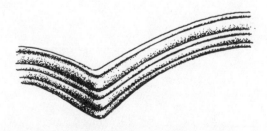

Left: a cross-section through 3,2,1 overpiping. The numbers indicate the size of the tube (tip) used to pipe the work.

Right: finished 3,2,1 piping has a 'step-like' appearance.

overpiped lines and the second single line. Lastly a single line is piped using the no. 1 tube (tip) to complete the graduated decoration.

Overpiping Template
Used for patterns on the side or top of cakes. The precisely cut template has the first line of piping placed very close to it. The template is then carefully removed and the remaining lines piped.

Secrets of Success
Each line must be dry before starting to pipe over it as there is a danger of the lines collapsing from the weight of the icing. Touch the surface of the iced cake with the tube (tip) to attach the thread of icing, lift the tube up to allow the icing to hang as it is guided along the row below. To finish the line, touch the tube (tip) down and the icing will break off.

Overpiping on Shells
The shell shape must be piped with a finely grooved tube to allow the lines of icing which are to be overpiped, to lay upon a smooth, even surface.

PAINTING

Painting is not as difficult as it may at first appear to be, particularly if the design is traced. The original picture can then be copied to reproduce the way in which the colours have been applied.

Brushes

The best quality brushes are sable which have soft bristles. They can be used to paint a fine point or used to cover a large area, depending on the size of brush. A nylon paint brush is also useful for fine lines.

To clean brushes, soak them in water and check that colour is not lurking in the base of the bristles. Smooth the hairs to a point and leave to dry facing upwards.

Mapping Pen

A nib with a very fine point, slotted into a holder. When not in use the nib can be reversed for storage in the holder. This gives greater control than a brush when drawing fine lines. Use with food colours, diluted with water if necessary. Often a picture can be given impact by outlining it with a fine dark line drawn in this way.

Surface

The iced surface should be smooth and dry. As the coverings are mainly sugar, the liquid used must be kept to a minimum, otherwise the surface will dissolve. Food colourings can be painted on pastillage*, sugarpaste*, run outs* and royal icing*. The last icing is the most difficult on which to paint as it is very absorbent and any mistakes cannot be erased without leaving a mark.

Technique

Lightly trace the picture on the surface. Hold the tracing paper firmly so that the design does not slip. Trace in the main details and outlines. Smaller parts can be painted in freehand. Paint in the light colours first as they can always be made darker, if required, at a later stage. Shadows give a painting a three-dimensional appearance. There must be a distinct difference between light and shade, perhaps in the way a flower petal turns.

When painting a scene with the sky in the background, make the colour of the sky on the horizon paler than it is at the top of the picture. This will give depth to the picture. Similarly, paint the smaller, farther-away lines of the painting in softer, hazy colours. Anything in the foreground will look sharper.

> **Remember . . .**
> *If the base colour of the cake or plaque is a pastel shade, this can alter the shades of the colours applied to the picture.*

Choice of Colours

Keep the colour scheme simple. On the comparatively small surface of a cake, a clear painting with few colours will create more impact than a multi-coloured painting. For example, use three colours and paint these in various shades. Alternatively, use two colours in the same colour range and the opposite colour in small quantities. For instance, pale and deep pink with a touch of violet.

Stir gold and silver non-toxic paint well as it tends to settle in the base of the jar.

> **Quick Tip**
> *Some colours take a long time to dry. Food colouring diluted with clear alcohol dries out quicker than that diluted with water.*

Painting Flowers

Keep the colours light, adding slightly deeper shadows. If lines have to be painted on the petals, start the line from the centre of the flower and gradually ease the pressure on the brush so the line ends in a fine point.

Portraits

Are for the professional or highly experienced, and artistic, cake decorator. Most figures applied to cakes are positioned facing sideways – this eliminates the need to obtain a life-like expression.

PAPERS, COVERINGS AND WRAPPINGS

An ever-increasing variety is available. Here is a brief guide to some of the most useful types. See also teflon-coated paper*.

Acetate: Firm, clear plastic sheeting, usually associated with use on overhead projectors. Acetate makes an ideal surface on which to make run outs*.

Cellophane: Transparent plastic wrapping, sold by the roll at cake decorating shops or stationers. Useful as a base for making run outs, also for making a see-through lid to cover delicate work which is placed in a box, particularly work which is prepared for exhibiting.

Embossed Silver, Gold and Red Papers: Obtainable from cake decorating shops and specialist stationers. Used to cover cake boards*.

Foil, cooking: Use to wrap rich fruit cakes* for storage only as an outer wrapping over greaseproof paper. Can only be used successfully as a covering for cake boards if thoroughly glued down; not recommended for special cakes.

Greaseproof Paper: Depending on the brand and where you buy it, greaseproof paper varies in strength. Look out for the strong variety for making piping bags*. Bags made of thinner paper may well burst during use.

Use for lining tins and for wrapping rich fruit cakes.

Non-stick Paper: Also known as baking parchment or non-stick cooking parchment. Use to line tins, make strong piping bags or for making small run outs. Do not use for making large run outs as it tends to wrinkle.

Rice Paper: Two thicknesses are available, the thicker type is usually available from cake decorating shops. Use as a base for making pictures in piping gel*. Liquid food colour and food colouring pens may also be used with care to paint on rice paper. Water will soften rice paper, so use a thin coat of piping gel or royal icing to attach it to a cake.

Roasting Film: This is easily peeled off dried run outs and lace* sections. Make sure the film is free of creases as they will weaken the run out.

Tracing Paper: Available from art shops. Use to make lasting templates and as a strong surface for tracing designs.

Waxed Paper: Traditional surface used as a base for piping run outs; however, the excellent range of alternative papers has overtaken this in popularity. There is no reason why waxed paper should not be used but some other types do allow for easier removal of the run out pieces.

Plastic Wrap: Dampen a piece and place it directly on royal icing* before replacing the airtight lid on the container to help retain moisture.

PASTILLAGE

Pastillage is a stiff white paste used for making flowers and models. Recipes vary but most include icing (confectioner's) sugar, white vegetable fat, water, gelatine*, liquid glucose* (clear corn syrup), gum tragacanth* and egg white. When cold, the paste sets hard but it will quickly become pliable once warmed and kneaded by hand. It can be rolled out extremely thinly, until it is transparent, when it can be cut and modelled into flowers. Once dry the paste resembles thin china – firm, yet brittle and easily broken.

> **Remember . . .**
> *Keep the paste covered at all times. It will dry out quickly if left open to the air. Break off only as much as needed at each time.*

Making Models

Roll the paste out, moving it occasionally to make sure it is not sticking to the work surface, and keep any dusting of icing (confectioner's) sugar or cornflour (corn starch) to a minimum. Excess powder will dry the pastillage.

Position the pastillage on a piece of glass or perspex, cut away any sections from inside the model and only then cut around the edge. This will stop the paste from distorting. Wipe the blade of the knife with a damp cloth occasionally, to prevent a build up of sugar. Leave on the glass or perspex to dry out in a warm room. After two days turn the pieces over to allow the base to dry.

> **Quick Tip**
> *Glass and perspex retain heat. If they are slightly raised up, this will allow the warm air to circulate and speed up the drying process.*

Colour

Can be added to the water in the recipe, but allow for the fact that the large amount of icing (confectioner's) sugar used, will reduce the depth of the colour.

Adding liquid colours will make the paste sticky. Paste colours are strong and only a little will be required. Use a cocktail stick (toothpick) to add colour. Many colours deepen on standing, therefore add the colour gradually and allow the paste to stand for a while before assessing the colour.

When dry, pastillage may be dusted with blossom tints* or it may be painted with food colouring.

Keeping Qualities

Well wrapped in a plastic bag, inside an airtight container in the refrigerator, the paste will keep for at least weeks. However, as the paste contains gelatine, small spots of mould can appear on the surface if the paste is old.

Freezing

Cut up, wrap well and freeze in an airtight container.

Pastillage Moulds

Pastillage can be used to make a variety of moulds. These will set hard and they can be re-used many times. For example, a firm object stamped into the paste will make an impression which can be left to harden. Decorations can be created by pressing paste dusted with cornflour (corn starch) into this mould.

PETAL POWDER

A white powder available from cake decorating suppliers. Add water as directed to make petal paste which can be rolled out or hand modelled. Sift the powder into a bowl. Add the water and blend with the tip of a round-ended knife. When the paste is made, use your fingertips to knead it into a smooth, firm ball. The paste is used mainly for making flowers.

Secrets of Success
Reserve some of the water suggested and add it later if needed. Adding icing (confectioner's) sugar to overcome the problem of having a sticky paste can reduce the stretching power of the paste. Always keep the paste covered. It will dry out very quickly if exposed to the air. Add a little vegetable fat if the paste is dry.

Colour
This can be added while making the paste. Once the paste is dry colour can be painted on, or blossom tints* may be brushed on.

Freezing
Any made up paste can be frozen in small blocks. They should be thoroughly wrapped and stored in an airtight container.

PHOTOGRAPHY

A camera with a zoom lens will produce close up photographs of cakes to show fine detail. A telephoto lens may also be used. Photographs taken with an ordinary camera do not show details of the decoration on cakes.

Daylight gives the best results – if possible take the cake outside. On a sunny day place the cake in the shade. Alternatively, place the cake near a window and stand to one side to take the photograph. If possible use a tripod or position the camera on a firm surface.

The side of the cake away from the window will be in shadow. To reflect the light back on this side, position a white surface (thin white card or polystyrene) just out of camera view.

Choice of Background
Having a background means that the cake will show up without the distraction of room details around. The choice of background colour depends on the colour of the cake. If possible, extend the background to cover the table area and drape it behind the cake.

Try not to take a photograph while the cake is on a silver stand, which is reflective and will blur the details.

Quick Tip
The wedding cake stand can be dulled for a photograph by applying a thin coat of window cleaning fluid.

PILLARS

Tiered cakes can be assembled on numerous types of support. Pillars are made of plaster, plastic or acrylic.

Hollow Plastic Pillars: For use when the cakes are iced with sugarpaste* and the soft surface will not take the weight of the heavy cakes above. These pillars disguise wooden skewers that run down their middle and it is these that take the weight of the upper cakes.

Clear Acrylic Pillars: Give a light, airy look to a cake and they blend in with any colour scheme.

Acrylic Separators: In various shapes to complement the design of the cake. These are clear stands which come complete with acrylic pillars to support and to spread the weight of the upper cakes.

Silver and Gold Pillars: The metallic colour should be repeated elsewhere on the cake or the shiny surface of the pillars can be too eye catching.

Plaster Pillars: Plaster will absorb water so they can be tinted to match a colour scheme by dipping them into diluted food colouring.

> **Quick Tip**
> *Plaster pillars need careful storage to avoid breakages.*

Using Hollow Pillars

Place the pillars carefully on the cake. Insert the wooden skewers, point down, through each pillar and the cake until they touch the cake board. Mark a line on each skewer level with the top of the pillar. Remove each skewer separately and cut level at the mark before replacing.

> **Remember . . .**
> *Each skewer should retain its original position once cut as the depth of the cake may vary from place to place.*

Glasses: For use on royal iced cakes instead of pillars. Small, sherry-type glasses can be used and they make an unusual talking point. They should be placed upside down, perhaps with a flower inside.

Tall Pillars: These are needed for large, deep cakes. Plaster pillars are obtainable up to 13 cm (5 in) tall. These give an imposing look to large cakes.

Tapered Pillars: Should be placed with the width at the base, allowing the narrow end to point upwards to the apex of the cake.

Royal Iced Cakes

The surface of royal icing* should be firm enough to allow any type of pillar to be used. It is sometimes the custom to attach the pillars to the cake with dabs of royal icing. However, the pillars can easily get knocked over and shatter the cake decoration. It also makes transportation difficult. Place the pillars in a separate box and position them carefully on the cake when it is being erected.

Placing the Pillars

Pillars should blend in well with other decorations and follow the shape of the cake. A small top cake will only need three pillars to support it. Place two towards the front of the cake and one in the centre back. The pillars must be the correct height to balance the depth and width of the cakes. Tall pillars, which are in proportion with large, deep cakes, look silly on smaller cakes. Always practise arranging the cakes on the pillars before the wedding day to ensure that the total composition is pleasing.

Design Idea
Narrow bands of ribbon or tiny sprays of flowers make an attractive decoration when wound around the pillars.

PIPED FLOWERS

These can be made well in advance and placed on the iced cake when required. Many different varieties of flowers can be piped, using the one petal tube (tip) and they will last indefinitely if stored in dry conditions. Warmth will not affect them but moisture could do so.

Use a small piping bag and ensure that the narrow end of the petal tube (tip) opening is facing upwards. The end of the paper piping bag must sit above the hollow at the base of the petal tube (tip) or the icing will creep through.

Use royal icing* which is well beaten and firm. Half a teacup of royal icing is sufficient to make many flowers. The icing should be stiff enough for the flower petals to hold their shape and for those of roses to stand upright. If the icing is too soft for piping roses, it may be the correct consistency for flat flowers which do not require the same stiffness to give the petals their shape.

Secrets of Success

Add ½ teaspoon albumen powder* to a small amount of icing (about half a teacup). Beat well, place in an airtight container and leave to stand for a few hours before using.

Drop Flowers

Are the easiest to pipe on non-stick paper*. Make sure the paper is secured down. Hold the tube (tip) vertical and very near the paper before starting to pipe.

Flat-surface Flowers

For example daisies, these are piped on a flower nail. The last petal is always the most difficult to pipe – hold the icing tube (tip) angled away from the first petal so as not to smudge the icing.

Roses

These can be made in two ways, either around a cocktail stick or piped on a flower nail. A third type of wired rose is made by the same piping technique used for cocktail stick (toothpick) roses.

Cocktail Stick Method: Use a wooden cocktail stick (toothpick) and make a small, tight coil of icing around the tip of the stick. Build up the petals on this base, overlapping them as you begin to pipe each one. Remove the rose from the stick by pushing a square of non-stick paper up the stick until the rose rests on the paper.

Flower Nail Method: Use a star tube (tip) to pipe a cone-shaped mound of icing on the nail and leave to dry. Pipe the petals on this base – these roses can be quite large.

Secrets of Success

Pipe a quantity of dome-shaped bases, leave them to dry, then pipe the petals around them when they are firm.

Wired Roses: Make a small hook at the top of a piece of medium gauge floral wire. Pipe a small coil of icing around the hook and leave to dry. Proceed to pipe the petals around the icing base, as for the cocktail stick (toothpick) method.

Colouring

White roses may be left to dry, then airbrushed* with different colours. Alternatively, flowers may be dusted with blossom tints*

when dry. Two colours of icing may be placed in the piping bag to make variegated flowers.

PIPING

Begin by practising piping techniques using buttercream*. It is easy to use and you will soon become confident about filling the bag correctly and being able to control the buttercream as you pipe.

Royal Icing
This should be well beaten and of the correct consistency. The smaller the icing tube (tip), the softer the icing so that it flows evenly.

Piping Bags
The size of the icing tube (tip) will dictate the size of the bag. For example, a tube (tip) with a fine point, which is used to pipe delicate embroidery, should be placed in a small bag.

Filling the Bag
First fit the icing tube (tip) into the bag. If too much paper is cut away from the end of the bag the tube may push out as you are piping. To avoid this, measure the point of the tube against the end of the bag and only cut away sufficient to clear the opening in the point.

Use a palette knife to put the icing into the bag. Place the tip of your thumb and forefinger together to form a circle. Gently drop the bag into the circle made by your finger and thumb. Place a dollop of icing on the end of the knife, then push it into the base of the bag. Withdraw the knife, using the pressure of your thumb to remove the icing from it as you do so. Do not overfill the bag. Fold the two sides of the opening into the middle, then fold the top edge over.

Remember . . .
Place the icing tube (tip) in the bag and make sure it fits neatly before filling with icing.

Piping Practice
• Use a dark, laminated board or place a piece of coloured paper inside a plastic folder as a practice sheet that can be wiped clean.

- Always try to work so that you are piping towards yourself.
- Begin all piping very near to the surface of the cake to ensure that the icing makes firm contact.
- Piping lines and dots provides useful practice: try to make the lines all the same length.
- Straight lines are easiest, so gain confidence by practising these first. The trick is to first make the icing grip the surface, then to continue squeezing the bag, at the same time raising the icing from the surface and moving along towards the required end of the line. To finish piping the line, lower the icing tube (tip) to touch the surface again. This way you will find that the icing falls in a straight line.
- Keep the opening of the icing tube (tip) free from excess icing which can blur the design.

Secrets of Success
If the line breaks, you may be using too little pressure as you pipe. If the piped line is wiggly, you may have used too much pressure.

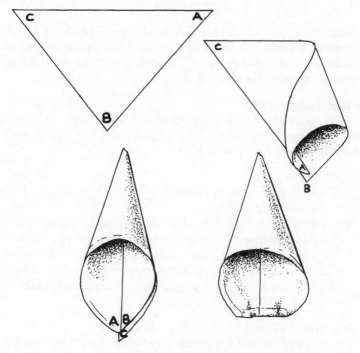

Making a piping bag.

97

Shells, Rosettes, Stars and Scrolls

For success these need well-beaten icing. Always re-beat machine-made icing by hand for a few minutes. Use strong non-stick* or greaseproof paper* for making bags as you have to apply some pressure to form the iced shapes. Always ensure that the edge of the paper is clear of the opening in the icing tube (tip) to allow a free flow of icing, otherwise the paper may obliterate, or at least smudge, the design.

If the point of piped stars is too peaked, immediately push it down slightly with a dampened finger or the point of a dampened paint brush by lightly touching the surface of the icing.

Shells should have a curved outline when viewed from the side.

Quick Tip
If the bag bursts just as you are nearing the end of piping a decoration, cut away the point of a new bag and place the torn bag inside it to finish the work.

PIPING GEL

A clear, sticky gel which becomes fluid when warmed in a small saucepan. When coloured it may be used for piping designs on firm royal icing* or sugarpaste*. Since it is not absorbed, the gel may also be used on rice paper*.

Brush Embroidery*

A small amount of piping gel added to royal icing gives it a smooth, elastic consistency. The icing does not dry as quickly, allowing longer for brushing it.

Creating Pictures

Pipe a fine dark outline in royal icing or chocolate* and flood it in with coloured piping gel.

A beautiful stained glass window design can be piped by outlining diamond shapes with royal icing or a thin line of chocolate and flooding in the sections with coloured piping gel. The surface of the gel dries and remains sparkling but it is soft to touch and eat.

Pipe the outline of a champagne glass in icing and make the contents and bubbles using piping gel.

Icing Tubes (Tips)

These are only needed for piping an outline. To fill in with gel, place it in a small piping bag and cut a hole in the pointed end.

Colour
Piping gel can be coloured with paste or blossom tints*. Stir the colour in well to prevent streaks; however, do not beat the gel or air bubbles will form in it.

PIPING STAND

Available from good cake decorating shops and suppliers, this is a metal stand with six holes to support piping bags. When using several bags fitted with different icing tubes (tips), or filled with different coloured icing, for piping intricate designs, the bags may be rested in the stand when not in use. A piece of sponge at the base of the stand is moistened and the points of the tubes (tips) rest on it to prevent them drying out.

PLAQUES

Piping on a plaque can have many advantages. For example, the plaque may be made well in advance and stored ready to be placed on the cake. It can be made of pastillage*, gum paste*, sugarpaste* or by making a run out*.

Several plaques can be made and the best one chosen for the cake. A plaque can be removed from a celebration cake and kept by the owner as a prized possession long after the cake has been consumed.

Run Out Plaques: These may be made in any shape or style and they have a slight sheen which looks very attractive.

Paste Plaques: Roll out the paste thinly. A cardboard template can be used to cut around with a sharp knife; however, a sharper edge is achieved by using a cutter, for example a pastry cutter or special plaque cutters. Leave the paste to dry in a warm place, turning it over after 24 hours to dry the base.

Design Idea
Raise a plaque on top of a cake to give it more impact. Pipe a few dots of royal icing on the cake, leave them to harden, then pipe on top of them again and carefully position the plaque. A plaque can be tilted forward slightly to display its content to best advantage.*

Writing on Plaques

If you are worried about writing directly on the surface of a cake, then write on a plaque instead. Make two or three extra plaques to give yourself plenty of opportunity for perfecting the message. Any unused plaques may be stored for future use.

Remember . . .
When writing initials or a monogram on a plaque, have sufficient room on all sides so that the lettering is not cramped.

PLASTIC ICING
See sugarpaste*.

PULLED FLOWERS

A wide variety of small flowers can be made using this method with flower paste*, pastillage* or petal powder*. The paste must be firm to withstand the pulling technique that is used to shape the petals.

Although many flowers have five petals, they can look quite different. It is the shape of the petals, the movement they are given and the colour applied that makes pulled flowers look individual and realistic.

Proportions

The size of the piece of paste used determines the size of the flower. A pea-sized piece of paste will make a flower the size of a primrose.

Shape the smoothed paste into a cone and skewer the wide end on a piece of pointed dowelling. Use your forefinger and thumb to thin the wide end of the paste by gently pressing the edge against the dowelling.

Make a number of cuts into the paste. The number of cuts equals the number of petals, for example five cuts will make a five-petal flower. The depth of the cuts dictates the eventual shape of the petals. Deep cuts will produce long petals which can be widened by rolling them sideways. When the cuts are made, remove the paste from the dowelling and model, or pull, the petals.

Pulling the Petals

Practise by making a flower with four petals first. Five-petal flowers are more difficult as it is harder to judge the cuts accurately. The paste can always be removed from the dowelling and the cuts made using a sharp pair of scissors.

The action used to pull the petals can be compared with snapping your fingers. Hold the petal between the forefinger and thumb, then flick the thumb and finger together, at the same time applying pressure to the petal.

Secrets of Success
To make accurately spaced cuts each time, mark five dots on the piece of dowelling.

Stamens and Calyx

These can be taped to floral wire and threaded through the flower when it is made, or the centre of the flower can be moistened and cut stamens placed in position. Stamens with stiff threads are easier to use individually.

The calyx can be painted on at the base of the flower. Start applying paint from the base of the flower and flick the brush up to obtain fine points at the end of the calyx.

REGAL ICE
One manufacturer's trade name for sugarpaste*.

RIBBON INSERTION

A pretty technique which has admirers of finished cakes debating over how the ribbon is slotted in place. This technique is often combined with crimper* work or brush embroidery* designs. The ribbon is usually slotted around the sides of cakes but it can look attractive as part of a top decoration. Ribbon insertion can only be applied on a coating of soft icing. Allow the sugarpaste to dry for a day before decorating with ribbon insertion.

Marking the Decoration
Measure the position where the ribbon insertion is required. Slightly below this point wrap either a ribbon or an even band of greaseproof paper* around the cake. Use this as a guide when making the cuts into the paste, to keep them in a straight line. Remove the paper or ribbon when the cuts are made. Ribbon insertion can also be applied in a curved design.

Ribbon Insertion Tool
Ribbon insertion tools or knives have a straight end on the blade to make cuts of an equal depth.

> **Quick Tip**
> *A pair of square-ended tweezers may be used to make two slots at a time in the paste. Wrap an elastic band around the tweezers to regulate the extent to which they can be opened.*

Choice of Ribbon
Stiff ribbon is easier to slot into the cuts. Floristry ribbon and double-sided satin ribbon are both stiff. Make sure that the ribbon and cuts are the same depth.

RICE PAPER
See papers, coverings and wrappings*.

RICH FRUIT CAKES

These can – and should – be made and stored for months before use. However, in an emergency they can be made shortly before a celebration without too much difference in taste.

Ingredients
Fat: Use only butter for a good flavour.
Sugar: Muscovado sugar is dark and moist with a soft, fine grain. It is ideal to give colour and flavour to rich fruit cakes.
Eggs: Use fresh eggs, preferably free range.
Flour: Use sifted plain flour with a small percentage of wholemeal flour to add texture and flavour. Using all wholemeal flour can make a cake crumble when cut.
Fruit: Currants will make the cake a deeper colour while raisins make it juicy.

Quick Tip
Gravy browning is sometimes included in recipes to deepen the colour of a cake. It can be rather salty and with the right ingredients it is not necessary to add browning. For example, treacle adds colour and flavour. Warm the tin of treacle in a saucepan of hot water to make the contents easier to spoon out.

Making Rich Fruit Cake
Warm the bowl and beater. Beat the butter until soft before adding the sugar. The butter and sugar must be beaten to a soft, light consistency.

Quick Tip
If the mixture is too firm, dip the base of the mixing bowl in hot water for a moment, then remove and continue to beat.

To smooth the mixture in the tin, repeatedly moisten the back of a metal spoon and smooth it over the surface of the cake. This will also prevent the surface of the cake from drying out.

Before baking rich fruit cake, lay a large sheet of greaseproof*

or non-stick paper* over the top of the tin, allowing it to rest on the lining paper. Carefully tuck the ends of the paper into the string around the tin. This cap of paper will trap steam and give the cake greater volume and a soft crust.

Secrets of Success
While the baked cake is still slightly warm pour alcohol, such as brandy, over its base and allow it to soak into the porous surface. This contributes more flavour than by adding the alcohol to the raw mixture.

Storing Rich Fruit Cake
When the cake is completely cold, wrap it well in greaseproof paper*, then in cooking foil and store it in a cool, dry place.

Remember . . .
Do not place cooking foil straight on a fruit cake. The acid from the fruit reacts with foil which will disintegrate on the surface of the cake.

ROASTING FILM
See papers, coverings and wrappings.*

ROLLED-OUT ICING
See sugarpaste.*

ROYAL ICING

The prefix 'royal' is said to have been bestowed after this icing was used on Queen Victoria's wedding cake. This type of icing was used long before that date. In 1609 a small cookery book included a recipe for making icing which used 24 eggs. After being beaten for hours it was applied to the cake with, 'a thick board, or a bunch of feathers'.

Making Royal Icing
The icing can be made with fresh egg whites or pasteurised dried powder, albumen powder*. The powder is easy to store and use, and it does not result in a surplus of egg yolks. Icing made with

albumen powder will be whiter than that made with fresh whites.

You may come across an instruction to leave fresh egg whites exposed to the air for a number of hours before using. This is because egg whites are composed of a large percentage of water, on standing some of the water evaporates leaving a stronger solution.

Lemon juice and cream of tartar are acids. When added to fresh egg whites they help to stabilise the egg foam and prevent it from collapsing. Many older books and professional reference books state that whites should be beaten in a copper bowl. The surface of the copper produces a stable foam.

Glycerine* attracts moisture from the atmosphere and when a little is added to royal icing it prevents it from becoming too hard to cut. However, properly made, royal icing will not dry rock hard. If it is beaten sufficiently it will be light when applied without being aerated.

Utensils

Any grease on the surface of a bowl or utensil will cause the whites to collapse. No matter how much beating is applied the icing will not be the correct consistency.

Quick Tip
Before making royal icing, rinse the bowls and beater with boiling water. Keep a few wooden spoons and a 13 cm (5 in) nylon sieve especially to use for making icing.

Making Icing in a Machine

Royal icing can be made using a heavy duty electric beater. The beater attachment must be used, not the whisk. This avoids the hard work involved in beating by hand, particularly if a large amount of icing is required. The drawback to this method is that the icing can be overbeaten. Keep the machine on the lowest speed. If the icing is to be used for coating a cake, make it two days before it is required so that excess air bubbles surface and are eliminated.

Secrets of Success
Always beat the icing with a wooden spoon for a few minutes after it has been made by machine. Also, whenever the icing has been left to stand, even if only for half an hour, give it another beating before using it.

Making Icing by Hand

This can be of equal quality to machine-made icing but it must be very well beaten. Whisk up the whites first and gradually add the sifted icing (confectioner's) sugar, beating well between each addition. The final consistency should be similar to whipped cream, white and soft in texture. Icing which is thick and leaden can be the result of repeatedly adding sugar without sufficient beating. Depending on the amount of icing being made, a few hundred separate beating actions may be required.

Royal Icing Mix

Packets of royal icing mix combine icing (confectioner's) sugar with albumen powder* and they are ready to mix with water. This is a convenient way of making up a small amount of icing. However, the icing does still require plenty of beating. For example, one manufacturer's instructions recommend beating by hand for 15 minutes – this is not an exaggeration and it is necessary for good results.

Consistency

For coating a cake, a softer consistency is required than that used when piping shells and stars. The icing should be similar to softly whipped cream. If it is too stiff add a little egg white or water. To stiffen the icing, beat in icing (confectioner's) sugar. Before adding extra sugar, always beat the icing, as this will stiffen it up slightly.

Quick Tip
If only a small amount of liquid is needed, drip tap water on the surface of the icing. Pour off the excess before beating. This method is preferable to adding teaspoons of liquid.

Blue Colouring

Icing made with fresh egg whites is not a pure white, therefore a small amount of blue colouring may be added to give the optical impression of whiteness.

Traditionally a blue bag was used for this. Obtained from a good ironmonger, a blue bag is a small cloth bag containing a blue substance which is intended for making laundry look white. Useful before the variety of soap powders now available was developed.

Using Royal Icing

To pipe stars, shells, rosettes, scrolls and flowers the icing should be firm enough to stand in a point. Dip the wooden spoon into the icing, then lift it to make a point or peak of icing. Hold the spoon with the icing standing up. If the peak stays upright, or droops only very slightly, it is stiff enough. If the peak of icing flops over quickly it is too soft for borders or for piping flowers.

Coating the Cake

Coat the top of the cake first. Use a stiff palette knife to spread the icing over the surface. Adopt a wave-like motion when using the knife. Push the icing with one side of the blade, then push the icing in the opposite direction with the other side. This action helps to break any air bubbles in the icing.

Wipe a metal icing rule with a damp tea cloth. Start at the far side of the cake and draw the rule across the icing at a 45° angle. Don't hurry. Correct any excess pressure on the rule that may result in the marzipan showing through. Remove any surplus icing from the edge of the cake.

Secrets of Success

Most cakes are given three coats of royal icing. Each covering will be smoother. When applying icing to the side of a round cake, it is helpful to use a turntable and to complete smoothing the coating in one movement.

When using the icing, keep the bowl covered with a damp cloth to prevent the air from crusting the surface.

Keeping Qualities

Place the icing in a clean bowl. Moisten plastic wrap under the tap and place it over the surface of the icing before replacing the lid. Store in the refrigerator for 1–2 weeks.

Icing Unusual Shapes

Horseshoe and Nought: It is difficult to apply royal icing to the inside curve of these shapes. Instead cover with a layer of sugarpaste*.

Hexagonal: To ensure that the angles on each corner are sharp, coat three alternate sides and leave to dry, then coat the remaining three.

Petal: On the inside curve of the petal shape, release pressure on the scraper to prevent the marzipan from showing through.

RUN OUTS

Also known as run ins, floodwork and colour flow. This technique can be used in many areas of cake decorating, for designs both large and small. Anything from a regimental badge or a swan to a three-dimensional picture can be created in run outs.

A basic run out consists of an outline of royal icing* which is piped around a tracing of the required design. Then the inside area is flooded with icing which is thinned to flow smoothly. The icing will dry with an attractive sheen on the surface. Once the icing has dried the run out can be used to decorate a cake or plaque*. Many complicated designs can be produced using this technique. Try a simple run out first, such as a heart or perhaps a butterfly. Don't attempt anything too intricate or a design with narrow areas.

Stages in Making Run Outs

The Design: Prepare a clear drawing. Cover this with paper that will peel off easily once the icing is dry – non-stick paper or wax paper. Cut the paper only slightly bigger than the drawing. Unnecessarily large paper can be a hindrance as a quick movement can catch the excess paper and break the run out. Stick the paper over the drawing with dots of icing or masking tape. Adhesive tape can be awkward to use. Place the drawing on a completely flat surface, preferably a piece of glass or perspex which will attract warmth and allow the icing to dry quickly.

The Outline: Use a small bag with a fine writing tube (tip). Keep the joins in the piping neat – they should lie against each other, not overlap. Flood in the area immediately. If the outline is left to dry it can break.

Flooding: Place the flooding icing in a small or medium bag. Cut a small hole in the tip of the bag to regulate the amount of icing flowing out and break any air bubbles in the icing. Air bubbles weaken the run out. Keep the tip of the bag down in the flooding icing to ensure a smooth finish and to fill all corners. If necessary, use a fine paint brush to gently ease the icing into difficult corners.

Drying: To obtain a glossy run out, dry it under the heat of a desk lamp with a flexible arm, in the sun or in a warm area. Stand the piece of glass up on small blocks to allow the air to circulate around the work. The drying time depends on the thickness of the run out and the consistency of the icing as well as the temperature of the room. Allow two days for the work to dry.

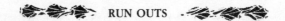

Making Stand-up Run Outs

Once dry, turn the run out over on its flooded side, pipe the outline and flood in the reverse side. Both sides will then be smooth and curved. If the piping bag used for outlining is made of silicone paper, simply place the whole bag in a polythene bag, seal and keep overnight.

> **Quick Tip**
> *A stronger run out can be made by outlining and flooding the icing on a base of dry pastillage*.*

Direct Run Outs

With some practice run outs can be outlined and flooded directly on the surface of a cake. This is a quick method which avoids breakages.

Curved Run Outs

You may want curved run outs to place on the side of a round cake. They can be made by securing the run out on a curved surface immediately it has been flooded. Apply overhead heat at once to crust the icing over before it starts to run outside the lines.

> **Secrets of Success**
> *The icing should be of a consistency to just flood evenly. Do not pipe too thick a layer within the outline.*

Figures, Crests and Pictures

To obtain a three-dimensional effect this type of run out is flooded in sections. Colour and thickness combine to give an impression of depth or to highlight separate areas. Leave the icing in each section to dry on the surface before attempting to flood an adjacent area. Figures can be made to look realistic by making the icing thicker in parts which would be nearer the onlooker, such as an arm or front leg which would be thicker than a back leg. These areas can be overpiped and flooded a second time once dry.

Lettering

Making run-out letters takes away the worry of having to pipe them directly on the cake. Large, clear letters are ideal for children's cakes. The dry letters are attached to the cake with small dots of icing.

Piping Gel
A piped chocolate or royal icing outline worked on the cake can be flooded with softened piping gel.

Chocolate Run Outs
Chocolate can be thickened (see piping chocolate*) and piped from a small bag. Use dark chocolate for the outline and flood in with a contrasting milk chocolate.

Secrets of Success
Flood the chocolate on paper with a shiny surface and it will set with a sheen. If set on matt paper the chocolate run out will be dull.

Simple, yet sophisticated, run outs can be made by flooding with dark chocolate and immediately flooding in light chocolate. Swirl or feather the two types of chocolate with a cocktail stick or the tip of a knife.

SEPARATORS
See Pillars*.

SMOCKING

Does not require a lot of skill to achieve a professional result. This technique is worked on soft sugarpaste*. Fine lines are embossed in the paste using a ridged rolling pin. The lines are pinched into patterns using a pair of plastic tweezers.

Quick Tip
If you want to practise before investing in the proper equipment, use a section of ribbed garden or plumber's hose, strengthened with a piece of dowelling through the centre. Try using metal tweezers if plastic tweezers are not available.

Making Sections of Smocking
Pieces of paste are embossed with the lines, then cut to size with a template. Moisten the surface of the iced cake and apply the section of smocking. Then pinch in the design, using tweezers, in various patterns based on embroidery.

Piping
A fine writing tube (tip) and royal icing* are used to decorate the paste with tiny 'stitches'. These stitches can be worked in one or more colours.

Secrets of Success
For effective results keep the lines of pinching close together. Have a fine, damp paint brush ready to eliminate any unwanted ends of icing.

SMOOTHER

Flat plastic utensil for rubbing over the surface of freshly sugarpasted cakes or plaques* to obtain a smooth surface. Available in a large flexible sheet or as a firm tool complete with handle.

Secrets of Success
Polishing sugarpaste* with the palm of the hand will produce a soft sheen but this cannot give the professional finish obtained when using a smoother.

SPACERS
See equipment*.

STAMENS

Can be bought in a wide variety of colours and sizes, from black stamens for the centres of anemones to glittery stamens.

Stamens with stiff threads can be placed into the throat of a flower without difficulty. Those with soft threads can be stiffened by dipping them into confectionery glaze* and leaving to harden. Alternatively, they can be taped on wires before being placed in the flower.

Japanese Stamens
Are expensive, extremely fine and difficult to handle. However, they do give a very realistic appearance to small flowers.

Quick Tip
Buy white stamens with a dull finish and colour them as needed by dipping them into food colours diluted with water. Curve the stamens over the end of the finger to make them look more lifelike.

STANDS

A wedding cake needs a special stand to enhance it and to add extra height. For an informal family wedding a large silver tray, perhaps with a deckled edge, will show off the cake.

Mirror: A mirror the same shape as the cake makes an unusual, reflective base.

Silver Stand: Either embossed with rows of beading or engraved with floral designs. They can usually be hired from a caterer or baker together with a matching knife.

Silver and Gold Plastic Stands: Are light in weight and attractive. However, they cannot compare with a real silver stand for quality.

Modern Stands: Can be bought or hired to support the tiers of the cake without the need for pillars. They are made from metal or acrylic in a variety of shapes. A popular form is the 'S' shape with either two or three platforms to hold the cakes. Other shapes and designs have staggered platforms.

STENCILS

The simplest form of stencil is a paper doiley through which icing sugar is sprinkled on the surface of a sponge cake. The following are all types of stencils which are useful for cake decorating.

Home-made Stencils: Use oiled parchment* or acetate* to make stencils, cutting them out with a sharp craft knife*. Study a book on the subject to decide where to place the 'ties'. These are the tiny sections which remain once the design is cut to enable the various parts to hold together.

Bought Stencils: Can be purchased from cake decorating shops or craft shops. Stainless steel stencils are long lasting, washable and flexible enough to remove easily.

Greetings Stencils: Offer an easy way of displaying a message on a cake. They save the trauma of worrying about spacing, writing style and the consistency of icing for piping. Stencils for greetings such as 'Happy birthday', 'Congratulations' and 'Merry Christmas' can all be purchased.

Picture Stencils: Depicting flowers and a variety of shapes. Use to add a quick decoration to a plaque* or cake top.

Using Stencils

Place the stencil on a dry iced surface. Use a palette knife to spread the chosen icing in a thin, smooth layer over the stencil. Carefully peel or lift away the stencil.

Colour can be dabbed through the stencil by using a small piece of natural sponge. Alternatively, it can be sprayed on with an air brush.

Secrets of Success
*The stencil must be kept perfectly still when applying
the icing or the design will be blurred. A small,
cranked palette knife makes the job easier.*

STRAIGHT EDGE
See metal rule*.

SUGAR

Sugar is produced from either sugar cane or sugar beet.

In the reign of Queen Elizabeth I, sugar was sold in 6.4 kg (14 lb)
loaves and pieces were broken off by using a small chopper.
Today there are many forms of sugar, which enables it to be used
to best advantage for cooking and icing.

Granulated Sugar: Ideal for general use and for boiling syrups.
Granulated sugar does not dissolve easily in cakes and its use can
result in white spots on the surface of cooked cakes.

Caster (Superfine) Sugar: A soft, fine sugar which dissolves easily
to give an even texture to sponges and fruit cakes.

Demerara Sugar: With large, golden crystals, this contains about
2% molasses.

Dark Soft Brown Sugar: Use to give colour and flavour to fruit
cakes.

Dark Brown Muscovado Sugar: This contains about 13%
molasses. It has a soft, fine texture and it provides colour and
flavour when making rich fruit cakes.

Icing (Confectioner's) Sugar: Made by milling and sifting white
sugar until the fine powder is obtained. An anti-caking ingredient
is added to keep the sugar flowing freely.

Golden Icing Sugar: A raw cane sugar which retains some natural
molasses. This makes delicately flavoured, fawn-coloured icing.
This is useful for buttercream but the colour is too strong for most
royal icing work.

Quick Tip
*Beware of wasps! They are attracted to sugar and
will quickly eat a hole into the surface of an iced
cake.*

SUGARPASTE

The original name, dating back to the 1600's. This is a soft, pliable paste which is rolled out and used to form a smooth coating on a cake or plaque*. Generally white, sugarpaste is easily coloured and it can be purchased in champagne and pastel shades. The champagne shade is a soft ivory which complements ivory-coloured wedding dresses when used on wedding cakes.

There is considerable confusion over the various names which are used for sugarpaste. Sugarpaste is particularly versatile and it can be used for covering cakes, making plaques*, modelling flowers or animals and making frills. The paste can also be flavoured to make cut out sweets or centres for chocolates.

Various Names
Fondant icing, rolled fondant, covering fondant, plastic icing, roll-out icing, moulding icing, satin icing, gelatine icing, mallow paste and pastello. Trade names include Regalice and Renice.

Home-made Sugarpaste
The paste can also be made at home but this scarcely seems worthwhile when you consider the time involved compared with the low cost and high standard of the bought varieties. If you do want to make sugarpaste, use a recipe that includes liquid glucose* and gelatine*. The glucose will give a soft, pliable paste and the gelatine will ensure that the paste will roll and stretch without cracking.

Applying Sugarpaste to Cakes
Only roll out the paste slightly larger than the cake. Excess hanging paste is heavy and it can cause splits to appear along the top edge of the paste.

Apply sugarpaste on the surface of the cake slowly and carefully to avoid trapping air bubbles underneath. Support the paste on a rolling pin or the back of your hands and allow it to lie gently over the cake. Follow these guidelines for success.
- Remove any large rings from your fingers.
- Use an extra-long, non-stick rolling pin. The smooth surface will not mark the paste and the extra length enables large areas of paste to be rolled.
- When covering Victoria Sandwich cake, use buttercream rather than jam to thinly cover the surface of the cake before

applying the sugarpaste. The buttercream will fill any uneven areas of cake to give a smooth coating.

• A thin layer of marzipan* under sugarpaste ensures a smooth finish. Brush a little alcohol over the marzipan before applying the sugarpaste so that the paste sticks down.

> **Quick Tip**
> *If cracks appear in the paste, polish it gently with the palm of your hand and the warmth should make the cracks disappear. If not, leave until the surface is firm, then blend in a small amount of soft royal icing* with the tip of a finger. Softened-down sugarpaste can also be used instead of royal icing.*

Colouring Sugarpaste
Use a cocktail stick (toothpick) to apply small amounts of colour. Liquid colours tend to make the paste sticky. Paste colours are strong and easy to use. Knead the colour into the paste. If a deep colour is required it is better to paint either paste or liquid on the surface of dry sugarpaste.

> **Secrets of Success**
> *To make sure that the colour is evenly distributed, cut the paste in half and check that there are no streaks of colour remaining. Home-made sugarpaste can be coloured by adding the colour to the liquid gelatine mixture.*

Storing Sugarpaste
Wrap the paste tightly in a polythene bag and store it in a cool, dry place.

Freezing
Sugarpaste-covered cakes may be frozen if necessary. Pack them in a large rigid container or box. Remove from the freezer 24 – 48 hours before required and place, still in the box, in the refrigerator. This allows the paste to thaw slowly and prevents a warm atmosphere from producing condensation on the surface.

Achieving a Sharp Top Edge
Roll out a length of paste, the same depth and circumference as the cake. Cover the paste with a strip of plastic of equal size, then roll both up together like a bandage. Unroll the paste around the side of the cake, using the strip of plastic to support it. The plastic also prevents the paste from sticking when it is rolled up.

TEFLON-COATED PAPER

A shiny surfaced, glass fibre material, which is washable and reusable. Obtainable from specialist sugarcraft shops and some kitchen shops or suppliers. This material is sold in sheets.

Uses
Lining Tins: When used to line cake tins it does not need greasing.
Making Run Outs: Made on this material the run outs detach very easily, avoiding breakages that can occur when releasing them from paper.
Piping Lace: It is a marvellous surface on which to pipe tiny lace pieces. A gentle movement of the paper is all that is needed to loosen them.
Flooding Chocolate: The shiny surface gives the set chocolate a sheen on the base.

Quick Tip
The paper is expensive but well worth the price. Remember not to cut it into small pieces, then find you require a large area, for example, for making a large run out. Two types of the paper are available, one darker than the other. Make sure you can see the outline of the design for the run out through the paper.

TEMPLATES

Use to mark patterns accurately on cakes. Greaseproof can be used to make a one-use-only template. For a re-usable template, use cartridge or tracing paper.

Top Designs
Cut out the paper to the same size as the cake. Fold the paper into two, then into thirds: this will open out into six sections.

To construct an eight-section template, fold the paper in half, three times. Cut the top of the paper into various shapes through all the thickness of paper.

Making a hexagonal template

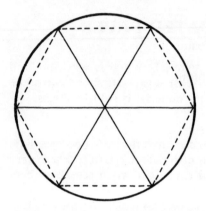

1 Fold a circle of paper in half, then fold it into three equal wedges.

2 Mark a straight line across the curved end of the wedge. Cut off the curve along the marked line.

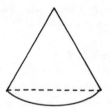

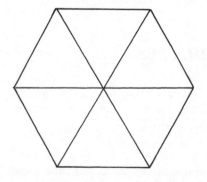

3 Open out the paper and use as a template for cutting a hexagonal shape from a slab of cake.

Secrets of Success
Cut a cross in the centre of the template and turn back the tiny sections of paper. This provides something to hold and to remove the template with when a line of icing has been piped around the perimeter.

Side Templates
Encircle the iced cake with a band of paper, then cut to size so that the ends meet. Remove and fold into the number of divisions required. Cut to shape and unfold.

Remember . . .
Measure the template after the cake has been iced. It will not be accurate if measured over the marzipan coating.

Hexagonal Shape
A round cake can be accurately cut into a hexagonal shape by using a template. Use a circle of paper the same size as the cake. Fold it into two, then fold the half circle into thirds, making six layers of paper. Draw a straight line across the top section of paper, across the curve. Cut off the curve using sharp scissors.

Secrets of Success
Before marking out template designs on the top of wedding cakes, work out the position of the pillars and allow sufficient space around them for the piped design.

TRACING PAPER
See papers, coverings and wrappings*.

TRANSPORTING CAKES

Travelling with cakes can be a nightmare. Most cakes travel well provided a few rules are followed.

Packing the Cake

A deep box with a separate lid is best for wedding cakes. Remind anyone who is lifting the box not to apply pressure to the sides but to take the weight on their hands under the box.

Placing a thin, folded paper under the cake board to raise it slightly provides room to grip the board when removing the cake from the box.

Obtain a wide, shallow and strong box from a supermarket for additional protection. Slit down both front corners, slide the cake box in and tape the sides together.

Small polystyrene blocks placed on either side of the board will stop the cake moving from side to side in the box. If the cake is too fragile to be placed down into the depth of a box, place the cake on the upturned lid and cover it with the base of the box.

Remember . . .
Hexagonal boards will require larger boxes because of the angles. Measure across the widest point from corner to corner. This distance is about 3.5 cm (1½ in) more than if measured from the straight edges. It is easy to forget such detail, only to find that on 'the day' the cake will not fit in the box.

Travelling by Car

Holding a cake box on the knee while travelling is not a good idea. If the car jerks, the cake may get damaged. Instead make room in the boot or baggage compartment of the car which is spacious and flat. A sheet of foam or 'plastic bubble wrap' underneath the box will help to counteract any bumps and a slightly damp tea-towel placed under the box will prevent it sliding.

Quick Tip
Sugarpaste and royal icing* do not melt in hot travelling conditions but a drop of moisture will dissolve the surface and leave a mark. Always keep cakes covered when travelling.*

TRELLIS

Fine lines piped in royal icing*. The lines can be piped straight on the top surface of a cake, over the top edge or as run outs

to be applied once dry. Trellis technique can also be used to make baskets and raised domes.

Technique
No. 2 icing tube (tip) is the largest to use and a No. 1 is preferable. The tube must always touch the surface of the icing to make a connection before starting to pipe a line. Always pipe the lines towards you, even if this means constantly turning the cake. Allow the icing to hang from the tube as you pipe so that it will fall in a straight line.

Trellis piped diagonally looks more attractive than straight down and across. Start in the centre of the design, work outwards to one side, then start again in the centre and work in the opposite direction. This method ensures that the lines are all at the same angle. The closer together the lines, the more effective the trellis.

Leave the first set of lines to dry before piping over them. If you make a mistake, remove the icing using a fine, damp, paint brush.

Overpiping
By decreasing the size of the icing tubes (tips), a second row – or more – of lines can be overpiped to give the trellis a 3 D effect. This can be enhanced by piping in colour, with each successive set of lines piped in a paler shade.

Trellis Around the Top Edge
Scribe two lines on the cake: one on the top surface of the cake and the second just below the top edge on the side, both an equal depth from the edge. Use these lines as a guide to help keep the trellis work straight.

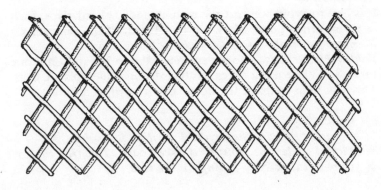

> **Secrets of Success**
> *Start by piping diagonal lines at 7.5 cm (3 in)*
> *intervals around the top edge. These lines will help*
> *to keep the piped lines at a consistent angle.*

Trellis Baskets or Domes

Trellis can be piped on a metal or plastic mould lightly greased with white cooking fat. Once dry, warm the mould. The fat will melt and release the trellis work.

TURNTABLE

A must for any serious cake decorator. Buy the best you can afford. Using a turntable enables a decorator to quickly reach any part of the cake. It is invaluable when applying royal icing* around the side of a round cake. As the turntable glides around the icing can be smoothly coated around the cake.

Tying ribbon around the cake is made easier on a turntable. With a flick of the finger you can see if the ribbon is level all around the cake.

Plastic Turntable: Light and suitable for lightweight cakes. Will not turn easily if a heavy cake is on it.

Metal Turntable: Heavy and long lasting, turns easily and is worth the cost. Keep out on the work top for easy access.

Tilting Turntable: Particularly useful when decorating the sides of cakes. Extending prongs clamp on the sides of the cake board. Then the turntable can be angled so that the chosen side of the cake is easy to work on.

Alternatives

It is best to avoid some of the recommended alternatives, such as an upturned bowl. They can be a hazard if the cake slips.

Floristry Turntable: A good second choice.

Folded Plastic Bags: More than one cake to ice and only one turntable? Place extra cakes, on boards, on folded plastic bags. This will help to make the board easy to swivel around.

> **Quick Tip**
> *A packet of icing sugar, laid on its side, can be*
> *placed under the front of a cake board. This tilts the*
> *cake to allow easy piping on the side.*

WAXED PAPER
*See papers, wrappings and coverings**

WEDDING CAKES

The ultimate goal for any cake decorator. So many people will view the cake, which follows the bride and her dress as the centre of attention.

Timing

Make the cake a few months before the wedding to give it a chance to mature and allow time to work out a design. Aim to have the decoration finished about four days before the wedding. This will allow time for final adjustments and for the bride to collect the cake in good time.

Work backwards when planning the timing:

- Finish cake 4 days before the wedding day
- 2 – 3 days for decorating
- 3 days for the sugarpaste* surface to dry
- 3 days for 3 layers of royal icing* to dry   base coat
- 1 day to apply a layer of sugarpaste
- 4 days for marzipan* to dry out
- 1 day to apply marzipan
- 2 – 3 days to make decorations, such as piped flowers, run outs, plaques or models.

This makes a total of nineteen days. Of course, experienced decorators can reduce this time, but it is useful to have some idea of how long the procedure can take.

> **Quick Tip**
> *Allow at least three to four weeks when making sugar flower bouquets.*

Size of Cakes

Cakes normally have a difference in size of 5 cm (2 in) between each tier. Up to 7.5 cm (3 in) between the size of the cakes is also acceptable, particularly if the cakes are deep. A two-tier cake looks balanced if the top cake is 7.5 cm (3 in) smaller than the base cake.

The bottom cake should always be deeper than the upper cakes. If the middle or upper cakes are as deep, or deeper than, the bottom cake, slice some of the depth away.

One-tier Wedding Cakes

Can be given extra height by placing on two boards, stuck together with dabs of icing. One board to be 7.5 cm (3 in) larger than the cake and the second board larger again by the same measurement. Ice and decorate both boards.

> **Design Idea**
> *A large round cake with a centre hole may have a bottle of champagne placed in the middle to make an eye-catching design for a one-tier wedding cake.*

Boards

If the cake boards are iced this allows the eye to flow from cake to edge of board without interruption and so gives the impression that the cake is larger. It also looks more professional.

Boards under tiered cakes should not be larger than the size of the iced cake below. This rule excludes cakes with run out collars, which should stand on larger than average boards because of the risk of damaging the fragile collar. In this case, the measurement of the board for the cake standing above should be the measurement from one side of the collar to the other.

Texture

Vary the texture of the iced decoration as a smooth overall finish can look very uninteresting. One way to achieve texture on wedding cakes is to add a fine pattern to the iced cake board by using a piece of natural sponge. Alternatively pipe a pattern of cornelli* work over it.

Design

See Pillars*. Graduate the size of piped flowers and other decorations on each tier of the cakes. Repeat shapes and colours to give a feeling of harmony to the design. The wedding cake is often seen only from a distance so the decoration on the side will be more noticeable than piping on the top surface.

The space left between the pillars on large cakes can often look bare. Remedy this by placing an upstanding model such as a pastillage* half-open ring box, complete with ring, a posy of flowers or a butterfly.

The top decoration should not be too wide and it should have some height to balance the appearance of the tiered cakes by bringing them to a point. Do not place flowers in a very tall, thin vase. They look insubstantial against the weight of the cake and, at worst, can topple over. A small silver vase, firmly packed with oasis, will safely display an arrangement of fresh flowers. The surface of the top tier is small, so allow a clear area in which to position the top decoration.

> **Quick Tip**
> *Why not ask a florist to make the top arrangement for the cake? He or she will know the scale of flowers to use in proportion to the container and the cake and a professional arrangement will look beautiful.*

Guide to Cutting and Portion Control

As a general guide, if each slice of wedding cake is 2.5 cm (1 in) square, in theory a 25 cm (10 in) cake should yield 100 pieces – but it never does! Slightly larger portions may be cut or part of the cake may crumble, so count on approximately 80 pieces.

> **Quick Tip**
> *To judge the approximate number of 2.5 cm (1 in) slices from a square cake, multiply the size of two sides together. Round cakes will always result in fewer slices.*

Cutting Cakes

If there is not a lot of top decoration on the cakes, it is easier to turn the cake upside down on the board and cut it from the base. Use a large, sharp knife and wipe it frequently on a damp cloth to remove excess sugar. This way less icing is shattered.

Square Cakes: Cut across one third of the cake and remove it from the board. This allows space to cut the remaining cake. Cut the cake across in 2.5 cm (1 in) wide slices. As each slice is cut, lay it along the cake board and slice it again into 2.5 cm (1 in) sections.

Round Cakes: Do not need to be cut into wedges. They can be cut in the same way as square cakes, although the rounded sides will give some smaller pieces of cake.

Another method of cutting round cakes is to cut a circle, going right down to the cake board, about 3.5 cm (1½ in) in from the top edge of the cake. Cut this section of cake into 2.5 cm (1 in) sections. Repeat with the remaining cake.

American Cakes

These are usually made from soft mixes or from a favourite recipe such as carrot cake. They are often iced in buttercream and frozen once the base coat is applied. The decoration is completed near the wedding day.

These soft cakes can be arranged in tiers using hollow pillars with dowels through the centre and separator plates to take the weight of the top cakes. Alternatively the cakes can be placed on thin cards of the same size, then stacked on top of each other. Each base layer of cake has four pieces of dowelling pushed through the cake down to the cake board, then cut level with the top surface of the cake. These take the weight of the upper cakes. Once in position any gaps in the icing around the bases of the cakes are filled and the remaining decoration completed.

To remove the cakes, ease a knife carefully under the thin cake board of the top cake, then lift away the cake and board.

> **Quick Tip**
> *If making the same design in rich fruit cake the dowels are not needed. Place the cakes on thin cake boards 2.5 cm (1 in) larger than the cake before applying the marzipan. For ease of working, position the cake and thin board temporarily on a large, thick board. Decorate each cake except for adding the bottom border. Stack the cakes on top of each other, then pipe around their bases.*

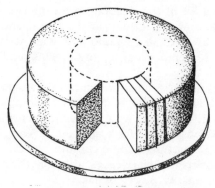

Cutting a round wedding cake.

WRITING

Although writing on a cake becomes the focal point of the design, this is one skill that is rarely practised enough.

Space
Consider carefully the amount of space available. Allow room on both sides of the name or message so that it stands out. If the message is long, start on the far left of the cake so that the whole width of the cake can be used. Decorate any excess space on the right of the cake with a small decoration, spray of flowers or a line ending consisting of tiny dots or scrolls piped level with the line of lettering.

Look at professional lettering and take note of the way it is achieved. Lettering on cakes often looks amateurish because of the wide spaces left between letters. The letters should be close to each other – almost touching – and the space left between words should be approximately the same size as the letter 'o'.

If the cake is large make the letters bigger. Run out letters look very attractive and they are easy to apply with tiny dots of icing. Keep the dots of icing small or they could ooze out from behind the lettering.

Centralising a Name
Count up the letters and divide the number in half. An odd number of letters is easier because the extra letter becomes the centre of the cake and the others are worked either side. Sometimes this does not work out satisfactorily as some letters take up more room than others. For instance, O occupies more space than I and two or three wide (or narrow) letters in a word can disrupt the spacing. Try practising the word before applying it to the cake. If not satisfied, measure the length of the piped word and start the piping on the halfway mark.

Style
One of the most difficult forms of writing is piping on a cake in joined-up writing. Notice the lettering applied to cakes in shop windows: it is usually written in capital letters. Quick to pipe and easy to read, capitals can be large or small. Over half the capital letters in the alphabet are composed of straight lines that are always easier to pipe than curves.

Secrets of Success
When piping a long word or unusual name, have it written out for reference. It is so easy, when concentrating on piping to miss a letter.

Timing
The writing is usually left as the last decoration to be applied to the cake. Reverse this procedure: pipe the message before the border decoration is worked. This means that it is far easier to pipe without worrying about damaging the top edge.

Direct Piping
Practise writing directly on the cake surface without pricking out the shape of the letters first as this can often result in a maze of bewildering dots. They can be particularly eye catching if the piped line does not lie immediately over them.

Use icing the same colour as the cake to pipe the lettering. Then if you are not satisfied, the icing can easily be lifted off using a small palette knife, without leaving a coloured smudge. Once perfect, overpipe the letters in a deeper or contrasting shade.

Quick Tip
Use a no. 2 icing tube (tip) for the base piping and overpipe using a no. 1.

Icing Tubes (Tips)
If piping directly on the cake, use a no. 1 icing tube (tip) which will give a fine outline and sufficient impact to be legible.

Easy Alternatives
• Imprint a greeting on soft sugarpaste* using an embossing set. Once the paste is dry, pipe over the impression.

• Use an alphabet set of cutters to cut out the letters in sugarpaste or marzipan*. Good for children's cakes. Marzipan is stiffer and will be released from the cutters more easily than sugarpaste. If having difficulty, dip the cutter into icing (confectioner's) sugar before using. The letters are made more interesting if the surface of the paste is textured with an embossed rolling pin first.

• Stencils* may be used to display a greeting. Place on a firmly iced surface of royal icing*, chocolate or sugarpaste.

• Pipe the greeting on a plaque*.

• Icing pens contain edible food colours and may be used to write on a strip of rice paper as well as on dry icing.